LOSING PARADISE

LOSING PARADISE

PAUL G. IRWIN

FOREWORD BY DENIS HAYES

SQUAREONE
PUBLISHERS

Cover Designer: Phaedra Mastrocola
Front Cover Photo: Digital Stock
    Corporation
In-House Editors: Joanne Abrams and
    Marie Caratozzolo
Typesetter: Gary A. Rosenberg

Square One Publishers
Garden City Park, NY
1-516-535-2010

Cataloging-in-Publication Data

Irwin, Paul G.
    Losing paradise : the growing threat to our animals, our environment, and ourselves / by Paul G. Irwin. — 1st ed.
    p. cm.
    Includes bibliographical references and index.
    ISBN: 0-7570-0003-7

    1. Animal rights—United States. 2. Animal welfare—United States. 3. Environmental degradation—United States. 4. Environmental protection—United States.   I. Title.

HV4764.I79 2000   179.3
                                  QBI00-360

Printed in the United States of America

10 9 8 7 6 5 4 3 2 1

CONTENTS

For my sons,
Christopher, Craig, and Jonathan.

ACKNOWLEDGMENTS

I would like to express my deep appreciation to several people for their help on this book, especially my friends and staffers at The Humane Society of the United States, whose expertise and assistance were essential for the completion of this project.

My assistant, Pat Gatons, handled many aspects of the book with her usual great competence; Deborah Salem, director and editor-in-chief of Humane Society Press, and Andrew Rowan tirelessly worked and skillfully guided the book through The HSUS' publication process; and Jan Hartke was responsible for producing and inspiring some of the book's best material.

Extremely valuable assistance and input were also provided by Patricia Forkan, John Grandy, Wayne Pacelle, Michael Fox, and Gary Valens, as well as Jonathan Balcombe, Rick Clugston, Linda Elswick, Susan Hagood, Sharon Geiger, Randy Lockwood, Rachel Querry, Brooke Sabin, Tom Rogers, and Teresa Telecky.

The book greatly benefited from the valuable material provided by my dear friend and colleague John Hoyt; Christine Stevens and Cathy Liss at the Animal Welfare Institute; The Public Employees for Environmental Responsibility (PEER); The Worldwatch Institute; The Fund for Animals; Thomas Berry; and *The Atlanta Constitution* columnist Tom Teepen.

Thanks also to my dear friend and respected colleague Lewis Regenstein, for his work in researching, organizing, and providing content for the manuscript, and to those who worked with him, John Elliott, Teresa Eddings, and Marion Cohen.

And our always gracious and brilliant publisher, Rudy Shur, and his excellent editors Karen Hay, Joanne Abrams, and Marie Caratozzolo were a pleasure to work with at all times.

Without the help and guidance of all of these dedicated people, this book could not have been produced, and I am more grateful to them than I can ever express.

FOREWORD

In the last half century, humans have acquired an unprecedented power to alter the face of the entire planet. Our species has always taken a toll on its immediate neighborhood. Three thousand years ago, humans changed the Fertile Crescent into a barren desert. But only recently have we acquired tools capable of delivering *planetary* impacts.

The first of these tools was the atom bomb. Before the Manhattan Project, the isotope strontium-90 didn't exist in nature. By the time the Russians and Americans got around to signing the atmospheric nuclear test ban treaty, every single animal on the earth—including every human—had strontium-90 in its bones.

Since then, the global assaults have multiplied. None is more dire than the epidemic of extinction now stalking every corner of the planet. Through the ecosystem destruction wrought by global warming, as well as through such long-established means as slash-and-burn agriculture, industrial clear cutting, and poaching, 6 billion human beings are shredding the great web of life.

Smaller numbers of Homo sapiens have been breaking a lot of little laws for a long time. Now the big laws, Nature's Laws, are catching up with us. We can't break Nature's Laws.

Paul Irwin has written an important new book on this new phenomenon, poignantly describing the common fate of humans and our fellow passengers on planet Earth. Irwin argues powerfully that the interests of humans and other critters are congruent. Indeed, he maintains, empathy for our fellow animals may help save us from our own desensitized selves.

Some years ago, I gave a talk in which I outlined some research at Stanford University which indicated that 40 percent of the net biological productivity of the planet is being used, directly and indirectly, by humans. In other words, 40 percent of the solar energy fixed by photosynthesis and stored in green plants was being harnessed to meet the needs of just one of the world's millions of species. I thought the number was absolutely shocking. As humans take 40 percent, we are leaving all the other animals on earth—combined—only 60 percent.

After my talk was over, a grizzled old guy from the audience came up to the stage to argue emphatically that God had given man dominion over nature, and that didn't mean just 40 percent. "I think we ought to get 100 percent," he said. I could only look askance at this man who thought that a world with no tigers or dolphins, no elephants or eagles, no bears or great apes could in any sense be a *better* world. Fortunately, the vast majority of people intuitively understand that this view is crazy!

Paul Irwin's new book argues that we humans can achieve a sustainable society only if we permit our empathy to extend beyond our own kind. In blunt terms, it is in our own narrow self-interest to genuinely care for animals as well as for people.

For example:

❏ We can save wildlife only by protecting the ecosystems that provide their habitat. Those same ecosystems enhance human well-being, purifying our water, producing oxygen, harboring medicinal plants, etc.

❏ Preventing cruelty to animals directly reduces the abuse of humans. There is a daunting statistical correlation between little boys who torture animals and violent adult criminals.

In short, humans cannot survive and prosper apart from the natural environment in which we evolved. We must cherish the whole rich tapestry of life, of which we are but a strand. We are arguably the most bold, audacious, clever strand—but we are still just one strand, and we depend on the whole fabric to ensure our well-being.

All of the world's creatures are dependent on our shared planet and on one another. We have a strong mutual interest in keeping that planet alive, intact, healthy, and vibrant.

Paul Irwin has shown us what we must do. I hope that this compelling work will inspire its readers to begin the task of building a truly humane, sustainable society—to repair our planet, to preserve what is left of the natural environment, and to make this a better world for all of earth's inhabitants.

Denis Hayes
President and CEO, The Bullitt Foundation
Chair and CEO, Earth Day Network

LOSING PARADISE

INTRODUCTION

As we begin the twenty-first century and the new millennium, one of the major issues facing America and the world is the place and plight of animals. For the creatures of the planet, the next century could be the best of times or the worst of times. The choice is ours. After the Great Flood, the Lord spoke to Noah about the birds, the fish, and "all that moveth upon the earth." "Into your hand they are delivered," said the Lord.

We must understand that the decisions we make in the next few decades will determine the fate not only of the world's animals, but probably of humans as well. And our past actions do not bode well for our future.

As the second millennium passed into history, it left behind a natural world reduced to a fraction of its former extent and beauty. The last few decades of the past century saw an unprecedented and unsustainable destruction of nature and wildlife by humans throughout the world. As the cartoon character Pogo said, "We have met the enemy, and he is us."

As environmental problems grow, overlap, and coalesce, we are facing a tidal wave of ecological challenges that undermine the natural world as we know it, and drown our efforts to save what we can. This tsunami threatens to sweep away what progress we so painfully achieved little by little during the nineteenth and twentieth centuries.

If we do not change our ways early in the third millennium, we will surely destroy much of those natural resources, systems, and treasures that make our lives enjoyable, worthwhile, and indeed possible. In fact, the fundamental challenge facing humanity at this time is the need to build a truly humane society. Such a concept includes respecting and caring for the lives of the other creatures with which we share this planet; taking into consideration the needs of future generations; and operating on principles of sustainability and concern for the natural environment.

At The Humane Society of the United States (HSUS), the group that I am honored to serve as president, we long ago realized that we could not fulfill our mission of protecting wildlife and other animals without also preserving the habitat essential to their survival. And that habitat—our planet earth—is now in jeopardy.

That is why The HSUS, operating internationally as Humane Society International (HSI) and EarthVoice, is working so hard to protect and save the ecosystems, forests, and other natural areas that are essential to the maintenance of a healthy planet. Save them we must if our own future is not to be lost along with the earth's natural biological systems.

That is also why we at The HSUS, as our name implies, are about the task of creating a humane society. While we are not so presumptuous as to think that we, by ourselves, will actualize this vision, we do believe that we, working with other dedicated citizens and groups, can be an important catalyst in mobilizing the citizenry of the globe in this noble effort.

And we *are* presumptuous enough to think that someday we can attain the reality of a truly humane society, and thereby provide the framework for a survivable planetary community that will protect, and not squander, the priceless natural heritage we have been given. It is simply inconceivable that, given what we know today, we would allow the destruction of critical biological systems that make life on earth possible.

Some of the tenets that lie at the center of our vision include sustainability, justice, compassion, and respect for those at our mercy. Although animals will be the direct beneficiaries, we will all gain from this effort. For it is increasingly clear that the world will not be safe for *any* of creation, including the human species, unless it is made safe for *all* of creation, especially those that lack power and influence. To strive to save our own species and those we find useful and appealing, while disregarding the fate of other life forms, is simply not a viable option in our interconnected world. For the passengers of Spaceship Earth, the natural environment, with its myriad creatures, is a "mission critical" system.

The conservation of our natural resources is thus the overriding issue of our times, but it must be a compassionate conservation, one that is inextricably linked to the humane treatment of all animals—including, of course, people. If we can build a truly humane society, tremendous improvements can be made in the lives of humans and animals. The development of such a society should be a priority for anyone who cares about the fate of the planet, and the well-being of animals, nature, and future generations of humans.

This book discusses the destruction of our wildlife and natural environment, and the cruel abuse of animals—literally by the hundreds of millions every year—by hunters, trappers, ivory and fur industries, and other traffickers in wildlife and their products. Most important, the book then provides suggestions for building a humane society. Not the animals only, but the planet itself is now in our hands. Let us make the right choice.

PART I

The Intrinsic Value of Animals

1. Loving Animals for Their Own Sake

At the dawn of a new millennium, humanity finds itself with virtually unlimited potential for doing good or doing evil, for building or tearing down, for sustaining or dooming our civilization. Humanity once again faces the choice presented to the ancient Israelites some 3,500 years ago, when Moses summoned the people to tell them the terms of their covenant with the Lord, saying to them, "This day, I have set before you life and death, blessing and curse; therefore choose life, that you and your descendants may live. . ." (Deuteronomy 30:19).

But we cannot choose life for some creatures and death and extinction for others, for we are all interconnected and dependent on one another. Only by appreciating the intrinsic value of all life can we hope to secure our own futures, that of our descendants, and that of the earth that sustains and nurtures the lives of all creatures.

BUILDING A TRULY HUMANE SOCIETY

As we enter the new millennium, any discussion of the threat to our planet and the plight of animals must begin with this question: How do we build and preserve our global civilization and the natural world upon which it is constructed? It is a question that could determine the future of our environment, our society, and ourselves.

First, we must halt the plundering of the planet, which, within just a few generations, threatens to squander and consume all of our natural inheritance. This inheritance includes the primeval forests, the indispensable topsoil, the spectacular wildlife, even the climate in which we evolved and on which we depend—including the world's protective ozone layer that makes life on earth possible. The damage that we do is not only a crime against nature and a sin against creation; it is also ecocide on a planetary scale, and, therefore, a sure path to the fall of the global association of human societies that we call civilization.

Finding the Unifying Principle

Halting the devastation of planet earth is an awesome undertaking. It will require the full attention and cooperation of communities and leaders across the globe, and a change in the way we have lately come to view religious and ethical obligations.

Humans place great importance on morality. We must therefore ask: What is our moral responsibility to the future—to our children and grandchildren, and to generations to come? Can a truly moral person condone, approve of, or participate in the devastation of our planet, or is this a violation of the standards to which ethical people should be held?

One of our first tasks, therefore, is to establish a unifying principle that can serve as a central organizing force for the global civilization—a principle based on morality and ethics, yet capable of uniting the great traditional pillars of integrity and virtuous conduct agreed upon by the world's major religions and philosophies.

One such unifying principle is the creation of a society that is humane in the broadest sense of that term, compassionate, sustainable, and just. Such a principle should be acceptable to all faiths and nationalities; to all cultures and races; and to people of good will of all social, economic, and ethnic groups.

This principle must also embrace the whole community of the earth—animals great and small, trees, plants, and myriad other life forms. It is a principle that recognizes the moral imperative of extending the circle of compassion ever wider until it encompasses all aspects of our lives, including how we treat animals and people;

how we produce and consume food, energy, and natural resources; and how we protect and care for the creation all around us. The principles governing such a humane society would ensure that every being, human and nonhuman, receives our concern, our respect, and our consideration.

Changing Attitudes

In order to create a humane society, we must learn to adopt an attitude of humility—a trait widely considered virtuous as a personal attribute, but rarely applied to the entire species. Yet given our long and bloody history of aggression, warfare, and cruelty, perhaps some humility is in order, as well as a determination to overcome our supremely confident, often arrogant belief that we are the pinnacle of creation.

It is this state of glorified self-esteem that led King David to praise the Lord for the exalted state of humans: "What is man, that Thou art mindful of him? . . . Thou hast made him but little lower than the angels, and hast crowned him with glory and honor. . . . Thou hast put all things under his feet. . . " (Psalms 8:4–6).

The smug, self-righteous, and almost universal veneration of humans over and at the expense of all other life forms is the source of many of our problems, and is leading us and the rest of the planet's creatures towards disaster. Yet we hear little protest from most of our religious and ethical authorities, many of whom justify and condone any abuse of animals and the environment if humans can extract some short-term benefit therefrom.

John A. Hoyt, formerly a Presbyterian minister and HSUS president, is an exception. He has observed that "man, the only living creature capable of reason (or so we like to think), deliberately torments, injures, and kills other creatures as though they were created to provide him [with] amusement and sport. Such thinking is the height of absurdity, and evidence of moral degeneracy."[1]

We need to rethink our immediately self-serving but ultimately self-defeating attitudes that place humans above and apart from all other earthly life forms. Just as all beings alive today have evolved from earlier life forms and have had to adapt to new challenges and changing environments, so must we evolve in our thinking and in our conduct. Perhaps this unifying principle of creating a humane society can act as the guiding light for what must become a new way of thinking and acting.

Signs of Change

It is encouraging that we have, in recent years, seen signs of change in some transcultural, transnational values—a renewed sense of the sacred in considering the earth's natural wonders. We see the governments of the world, at their highest levels, rhetorically committing themselves to conservation, sustainability, and protection of the natural environment. But whether stirring words will result in real action remains to be seen. So far, they have not, and we must soon find a way to translate sentiment into substance. In 1958, anthropologist Margaret Mead said that because of the human tendency towards self-destruction, we need a new pattern for organizing the management of civilization:

> The readings of history and anthropology in general give no reason to believe that societies have built-in self-preservation systems. And therefore we can't say that man will be sensible enough not to destroy himself. He never has been sensible enough not to destroy himself, but he lived in small groups, so that when he destroyed himself he didn't destroy everybody. So the necessity for new inventions for the conduct of the world cannot possibly be over-emphasized.[2]

LOVING ANIMALS FOR THEIR OWN SAKE

The first and most important step in creating a truly humane society is to recognize the intrinsic value of nature and animals. We must embrace the concept that animals and other life forms should be respected, protected, and cherished—not because they may be useful to humans, but for their own sake.

Although appreciating animals for their own worth may seem to some to be a radical or revolutionary concept, there is really nothing new or extreme about it. Indeed, such teachings are found and even emphasized in some of the earliest and most revered writings of humanity.

The Teachings of the Bible

In numerous passages, the Bible stresses mankind's obligations to respect and protect animals, to show a reverence for nature, and to act as a caretaker of the environment. In the first chapter of Genesis, before humans had yet appeared, the Lord characterizes as "good" in themselves the various components of nature that He has created. These include the land, the grass, the trees, and the "swarms of living creatures"—birds, whales, cattle, "everything that creepeth upon the ground," and the other "beasts of the earth." After each of the acts of creation, Genesis tells us, "God saw that it was good."

Many other Biblical passages characterize animals as worthy of consideration for their own sake. Even the holiest of the Mosaic laws—the Ten Commandments—forbids the working of farm animals on the Sabbath. Humans are commanded periodically to leave grain in their fields for wildlife, "for the beasts that are in thy land" (Leviticus 25:4–7; Exodus 23).

The story of Job, who was a fine naturalist, makes it clear that the Lord loves the land for its own sake, and not just as a resource for humans. Speaking from the whirlwind, the Lord tells Job how He "causes it to rain on the earth, where no man is: on the wilderness, wherein there is no man; to satisfy the desolate and waste ground; and to cause the bud of the tender herb to spring forth" (Job 38:26–27). Job stresses over and over again the virtues of living in harmony with nature, which, he argues, contains great wisdom for those willing to study it.

Compassion towards animals is another recurring theme of the Bible. The book of Proverbs (12:10) suggests that "righteous" people are kind to animals, while the "wicked" are cruel to those creatures under their care: "A righteous man has regard for the life of his beast, but the tender mercies of the wicked are cruel." In the book of Ecclesiastes, we are told that the human conceit of superiority over animals is mere vanity: "Yea, they have all one breath; so that man hath no preeminence above a beast; for all is vanity. All go unto one place; all are of the dust, and all return to dust" (Ecclesiastes 3:19–21).

In the New Testament, Jesus preaches that God loves even the least of His creatures, saying, "Are not five sparrows sold for two pennies? And not one of them is forgotten before God" (Luke 12:6; see also Matthew 10:29).

Centuries-Old Reverence for Nature

For centuries, leading theologians and religious figures have embraced the idea that nature and animals have an innate worth that compels us to respect and revere the Creation. The early Christian saints are often described as befriending and defending innocent animals and developing close relationships with such creatures. The significance of these stories, many doubtless apocryphal, was noted by Irish historian W.E.H. Lecky (1838–1903). In his classic work *History of European Morals from Augustus to Charlemagne* (1869), Lecky writes: "These legends are worthy of special notice in moral history as representing the first, and at the same time one of the most striking, efforts ever made in Christendom to inculcate a feeling of kindness and pity towards the brute creation."[3]

Such revered saints as Benedict, Columba, Cuthbert, Giles, Jerome, Meinrad, Patrick, and literally hundreds of others were legendary for their love of and compassion towards animals. The best known of all these saints is Saint Francis of Assisi (1182–1226), who founded the Franciscan Order and was canonized in 1228. Stories of his acts of kindness to animals are legion, and he is said to have preached to the animals and the flowers, with the birds responding to his sermons by chirping and flapping their wings in ecstasy. He is purported to have removed worms from the road to prevent their being crushed, and to have brought wine and honey to hungry bees in winter.[4, 5]

The number of such anecdotes, regardless of their veracity, makes it clear that the attitudes of some of the Church's most revered figures were marked by compassion and respect for the creatures of the earth.[6]

More recently, Nobel laureate Dr. Albert Schweitzer (1875–1965) not only preached but lived by the humane ethic of "reverence for life" for all creatures. A Protestant clergyman and medical missionary, Schweitzer wrote that "sympathy with animals, which is so often represented as sentimentality, [is] a duty which no thinking man can escape":

> A man's religion is of little value unless even seemingly insignificant creatures benefit from it. A truly religious man does not ask how far this or that life deserves sympathy as valuable in itself. Nor how far it is capable of feeling. To him, life as such is sacred. The countryman who has mowed down a meadow as fodder for his cows should take care that on his way home he does not, in wanton pastime, cut off the head of a single flower growing on the edge of

the road, for in doing so he would injure life without being forced to do so by necessity.[7, 8]

Compassion was central to Schweitzer's code of morality. He argued, "A man is truly ethical only when he obeys the compulsion to help all life which he is able to assist, and shrinks from injuring anything that lives." Schweitzer did not place a higher value on creatures considered useful to humans, but considered all life forms to be worthy of consideration:

> In the past, we have tried to make a distinction between animals which we acknowledge have some value, and others which, having none, can be liquidated when we wish. This standard must be abandoned. Everything that lives has value simply as a living thing, as one of the manifestations of the mystery of life.[9]

The famous American naturalist John Muir (1838–1914), who founded The Sierra Club in 1892 and led the fight to establish Yellowstone National Park in 1889, campaigned for a spiritually based ethic for preserving the natural environment. In his years of exploring the American wilderness from Indianapolis through California and Alaska, he never carried a gun. He detested hunting, believing that "making some bird or beast go lame the rest of its life is a sore thing on one's conscience, at least nothing to boast of, and has no religion in it."[10]

Muir also respected the right of all creatures to exist, even those considered by human standards to be ugly and dangerous. Once, after a close call with an alligator, he wrote:

> Doubtless these creatures are happy, and fill the place assigned to them by the great Creator of us all. Fierce and cruel they appear to us, but beautiful in the eyes of God. . . . How narrow we selfish, conceited creatures are in our sympathies. How blind to the rights of all the rest of creation.[11]

During the last two decades of the twentieth century, a spiritually based appreciation for animals and nature took root within the religious community, and many groups, leaders, and individuals called for society to adopt an ethic of respect for other life forms. One of the first clergymen to view environmental problems as moral issues was the Right Reverend Robert McConnell Hatch, who, as the suffragan bishop of Connecticut, published in 1967 in the *Atlantic Naturalist* his "Cornerstones for a Conservation Ethic":

> The cause of conservation involves man's soul. It is a spiritual choice, grounded in ethics, and its roots are in the Bible. Conservation teaches the principles of wise stewardship. It is profoundly ethical because it counsels foresight in place of selfishness; vision in place of greed; reverence in place of destructiveness. . . .[12]

Hatch believed that the earth and its natural treasures—"the trackless forests, the rivers that wind across our continent, the marsh lands, the prairies and the deserts"—were a sacred trust that humans had no right to use up or destroy:

> All of these things have been loaned to man as a trust. None of it really belongs to him. His days are as grass, and when the span of his life is over, he is the owner of nothing. He is called to be a steward of the riches of the earth, leaving them as a goodly inheritance to his children.[13]

Hatch understood that humans "do not really stand alone, but are a part of an intricate web of life in which all the parts are related to one another, and where the well-being of one part depends on the well-being of all." He repeatedly stressed that "conservation, in its essence, is a moral and spiritual matter":

> Man . . . is here only as a steward, and he will be judged by the way he treats what has been loaned to him. This not only involves the use of our land and resources for the sake of the present generation, but it also upholds the rights of those who will inherit the earth from us. If we leave them nothing but desecration, we shall be judged accordingly, and the judgment will be a moral one.[14]

Reverend Andrew Linzey, a Church of England theologian and author of *Christianity and the Rights of Animals* (1987), has written extensively on Christian theology and human obligations to respect the intrinsic rights of other life forms. "Animals are valuable in themselves by virtue of their creation by God," he writes. Linzey adds that injuring animals "is a practical denial of their intrinsic value. Animals belong to God in a way that makes their significance and value more fundamental even than human artistic creations. . . ." [15]

In support of his argument, Linzey cites no less an authority than the Archbishop of Canterbury, who has reasoned:

> If [Creation] exists for God's glory, that is to say, it has a meaning and worth beyond its meaning and worth as seen from the point of view of human utility. It is in this sense that we can say that it has intrinsic value. To imagine that God has created the whole universe solely for man's use and pleasure is a mark of folly.[16]

Philosopher-theologian Charles Birch writes that the integrity of Creation must involve recognition of the "intrinsic value of every living creature and the maintenance of the integrity of the relations of each creature to its environment."[17]

Charles G. Spencer, chairman of the National Ecology Commission of the Secular Franciscan Order, would agree that we cannot rank life forms in order of importance. He calls pesticides "a condemnation of life . . . [that] keep creation at bay, and God out, raining violence upon creation, because of fear and vanity. To judge the value of life is to question the Giver of life."[18]

Modern-Day Theologians

Today, many religious leaders and groups are urging that humans show consideration for the intrinsic value of other life forms with which we share the earth. This trend has been noted by my friend and colleague John A. Hoyt, who, during his almost three decades as president of The HSUS, strongly promoted this concept. He observes that "central to the emerging world ethic is the recognition that nature (including animals) has integrity and value independent of its utility to humans. . . . We are the children of creation. To us has been passed the awesome responsibility of preserving its inherent value and worth."[19]

No less a figure than Pope John Paul II has endorsed an attitude of respect for nature. He affirms Saint Francis as the patron saint of ecology, and suggests that Creation has value in and of itself, stating that "the aesthetic value of creation cannot be overlooked." He asserts, "Our very contact with nature has a deep restorative power; contemplation of its magnificence imparts peace and serenity. The Bible speaks again and again of the goodness and beauty of creation, which is called to glorify God."[20]

John Hart, author of *The Spirit of the Earth: A Theology of the Land*, writes that appreciating "the inherent worth of all creatures" could help save us from disaster:

> If we view the earth with anthropocentric eyes, then all creatures will be seen has having been placed here for human benefit, and all creation will be viewed as imperfect until human work transforms it to serve mankind. Should this perspective prevail, exploitation of all the Earth's goods [including] all the Earth's life forms, will be the more readily justified, with potentially catastrophic consequences. [21]

But it is not just Christian theologians who advocate a reverence for animals and nature; the other great religions of the world, especially in the East, also teach appreciation for their intrinsic value. Unfortunately, as with Christianity, the followers of these faiths often ignore or are unaware of their traditions of reverence for life. But these tenets are there for anyone willing to see them.

Judaism—A Tradition of Compassion

Beginning almost four thousand years ago, the teachings and laws of Judaism strongly emphasized kindness to animals and respect for nature. Indeed, an entire code of laws relates to preventing "the suffering of living creatures." Jewish prayers, legends, and literature contain countless stories and teachings emphasizing the importance of the natural world and animals as manifestations of the greatness and love of the Lord for His Creation. As *The Jewish Encyclopedia (Encyclopedia Judaica)* explains:

> Moral and legal rules concerning the treatment of animals are based on the principle that they are part of God's creation toward which man bears responsibility. The Bible . . . makes it clear not only that cruelty to animals is forbidden, but also that compassion and mercy to them are demanded of man by God. . . . In later rabbinic literature . . . great prominence is also given to demonstrating God's mercy to animals, and to the importance of not causing them pain.[22]

In Jewish tradition, someone cannot be considered righteous who does not treat animals with compassion. Rabbinical law requires that a person feed his animals before sitting down to eat and ordains that "a good man does not sell his beast to a cruel person." Fundamental tenets of Judaism include various ordinances requiring respect and protection for trees, for the land, and for nature in general, and forbidding abuse and pollution of the environment.[23, 24]

Hinduism—Avoid Harm to Living Creatures

Hinduism, the primary religious culture of India, takes very seriously the sacredness of all life, which can be summed up in the proverb: "Do not kill any animal for pleasure; see harmony in nature; and lend a helping hand to all living creatures."

A fundamental tenet of Hinduism is the principle of *ahimsa*— avoiding harm to living creatures. Since Hindus believe in reincarnation, all living creatures enjoy a kinship with one another, and are worthy of life and respect. Indeed, the status of one's next life is determined to a great degree by how well one treats other creatures in his life.

Hinduism also accords great importance to the sanctity of nature and to "mother earth," as is described in the September 1986 "Hindu Declaration on Nature":

> The Hindu viewpoint on nature . . . is permeated by a reverence for life, and an awareness that the great forces of nature—the earth, the sky, the air, the water and fire—as well as various orders of life including plants and trees, forests and animals, are all bound to each other within the great rhythms of nature.[25]

In Hindu scriptures, trees and forests are accorded special reverence, and flowering trees often become places of worship.

Jainism—Respect All Living Creatures

No people in India are more economically and educationally successful than members of the ascetic religion of Jainism—and none are stricter in their commitment to avoid doing harm to living creatures of every type. Devout Jainist monks have such a strong reverence for life that they wear a cloth over their mouths and sweep the path in front of them to avoid inhaling or crushing insects. Not only are Jains strict vegetarians, but they also avoid foods that contain "lower" life forms such as mold and yeast.[26, 27, 28]

The Jains are extremely prosperous and are known for their generous support of charitable causes. Throughout India, they operate hospitals and sanctuaries for sick, injured, and unwanted animals. Regrettably, many Jains and Hindus will not euthanize terminally sick and injured animals because they believe that killing violates *ahimsa*, and that such an act makes the perpetrator spiritually impure. The HSUS's senior scholar Dr. Michael Fox calls such an attitude "regrettable," since "the doctrine of *ahimsa* takes precedence over *dayakriya*—compassionate action. This in part accounts for much animal suffering in India, especially of 'sacred' cows."[29]

Buddhism—Compassion for All Living Things

Buddha summarized Buddhism's most important principle as having "a loving, compassionate heart for all creatures." Like Hinduism, Buddhism embraces the concept of *ahimsa*, a reverence for life stemming from the unity of all living creatures. Because all life forms are interrelated and part of a larger unified life force, to harm any creature is to hurt one's own self and all life.[30]

The Buddhist spiritual leader Holiness Tenzin Gyatso, the fourteenth Dalai Lama, writes in his book *A Human Approach to World Peace*, "Life is as dear to a mute animal as it is to any human being":

> Whether they belong to more evolved species like humans, or simpler ones such as animals, all beings primarily seek peace, comfort, and security. . . . Even the simplest insect strives for protection from dangers that threaten its life. Just as each of us wants to live and does not wish to die, so it is with all other creatures in the universe.[31]

Buddhism manifests a deep regard for nature's beauty and diversity, especially trees and forests, which are accorded strict protection. In fact, Buddhist monks are forbidden to cut down or mutilate trees.[32]

Islam—Respect for Animals and Nature

Although the humane and compassionate aspects of Islam are not widely appreciated, the Muslim faith strictly prohibits cruelty to animals and desecration of the environment, and requires that Muslims show respect and compassion for nature and animals. Indeed, the religion's founder, the prophet Mohammed (570–632), taught that animals should always be treated with reverence and respect. He is often quoted as stating "God (Allah) says, 'There is not an animal [that lives] on earth, nor a being that flies on its wings, but [forms part of] communities like you.'"[33]

The holiest of the Muslim scriptures, the Koran, quotes Mohammed as saying, "A good deed done to an animal is as meritorious as a good deed done to a human being, while an act of cruelty to an animal is as bad as an act of cruelty to a human being." "Islamic Principles for the Conservation of the Natural Environment," a 1983 booklet published in Saudi Arabia, says of wildlife, "Islam emphasizes all measures for the survival and perpetuation of these creatures so that they can fully perform the functions assigned to them, for He considers them living communities, exactly like mankind."[34]

Other Religions and Cultures

Many other religions and cultures—including the Baha'is of Iran, Native Americans, Amazon Indian tribes, and other indigenous peoples—recognize in a simple but profound way the sanctity of nature and the intrinsic value of animals. According to Iroquois clan Chief Oren Lyons, "Indigenous people have a long-term moral perspective on the earth and its life. We have no complex answers, but only the simple principle of respect for all life, for the trees, the rivers, the fish, the animals. . . . The principles of life remain simple. If we break those rules . . . , we break the cycle of life, and life will disappear."

This deep-seated veneration of the earth, so strongly felt by the ancients and aboriginal peoples, has been embraced by some modern-day scholars. Dr. Michael Fox writes of "the Creation-centered spirituality and ethics of panentheism," which he defines as "a reverence for the sacredness of Earth and for the inherent divinity of animals and all living beings":

A panentheistic worldview lies deep in our psyches, in our collective memory, psychohistory and instinctive longing for that time when we danced with wolves and sang to the

stars. Panentheism was the primal key, not back to Eden nor
on to paradise, but to living in communion. Through panentheistic sensibility, our ancestors conceived a Covenant
between Creator and Creation that humankind is enjoined,
spiritually and ethically, to uphold.[35]

There is, thus, a strong foundation of "reverence for life" in all
of the world's major faiths. And even though many people refuse
to recognize the ancient precepts of their religions, these precepts
hold tremendous potential to stimulate a spiritually based humane
and ecological ethic throughout the world.

The World of Science

Some of the best minds of science have also perceived the importance of appreciating the intrinsic value of animals and nature, and
warned of the consequences of wantonly destroying life forms so
closely linked to our own.

The renowned English scientist Charles Darwin (1809–1882)
strongly promoted kindness to animals and worked to help pass
England's 1876 Cruelty to Animals Act, which regulated laboratory research on animals. His revolutionary theory of evolution
helped corroborate scientifically the religious writings of earlier
humanitarians that cited the kinship between humans and animals. His theory was also instrumental in refuting the prevailing
view of animals as machines devoid of feelings and intelligence.
Since he was perhaps the most important and acclaimed scientist
of his times, his research on the amazing similarities between
humans and other mammals concerning intelligence, emotions,
and social structure could not be as easily dismissed as were similar writings of others with less impressive scientific credentials.

Darwin did not agree with David's description in the Eighth
Psalm of man as "a little lower than the angels." He saw humans
as closer to animals than angels, writing in his diary that "man, in
his arrogance, thinks himself a great work, worthy of the interpo-
sition of a deity. More humble and, I believe, true to consider him
created from animals."[36]

Over three decades later, in *The Descent of Man* (1871), Darwin
wrote that "the difference in mind" between humans and animals
"certainly is one of degree and not of kind."[37] He further stated, "We
have seen that the senses and intuitions, the various emotions and

faculties, such as love, memory, attention, curiosity, imitation, reason, etc., of which man boasts, may be found in an incipient, or even sometimes in a well-developed condition, in the lower animals."[38]

Darwin felt strongly that humans were obliged to treat animals with compassion, and he once stated that "sympathy with the lower animals is one of the noblest virtues with which man is endowed."

Another scientific genius who perceived the inner worth of animals was *Time* magazine's "Man of the Century," Albert Einstein (1879–1955), who wrote, "Our task must be to free ourselves by widening our circle of compassion to embrace all living creatures, and the whole of nature in its beauty." He predicted, "There will come a day when men such as myself will view the slaughter of innocent creatures as horrible a crime as the murder of his fellow man."[39]

The late author-astronomer Carl Sagan, Director of the Laboratory for Planetary Studies at Cornell and a leading consultant to NASA on several expeditions, wrote frequently of the wonders of nature and animals. In his international bestseller *Cosmos*, he wrote that humankind's dominance of the planet should be attributed more to a quirk or accident of evolution than to human excellence:

> Just sixty-five million years ago, our ancestors were the most unprepossessing of mammals—creatures with the size an intelligence of moles or tree shrews. . . . It was some horde of furry little mammals who hid from the dinosaurs, colonized the treetops and later scampered down to domesticate fire, invent writing, construct observatories, and launch space vehicles. If things had been a little different, it might have been some other creature whose intelligence and manipulative ability would have led to comparable accomplishments.[40]

At the January 1990 Global Forum of Spiritual and Parliamentary Leaders, held in Moscow, Sagan organized and presented a statement entitled "Preserving and Cherishing the Earth." Signed by thirty-two leading scientists, the document referred to the "profound experiences of awe and reverence before the universe" that many of the scientists had experienced. Further, it urgently requested an end to "crimes against creation" and a joint commitment between science and religion "to preserve the environment of the earth."[41]

FALLING IN LOVE WITH THE EARTH

In the final analysis, if we are to save the earth, we must begin to regard it as a treasure to cherish instead of a resource to exploit. As Jan A. Hartke, executive director of EarthVoice, explains:

> If we are to succeed in saving the beauty, diversity, and life of our planet, people must fall in love with the earth and the animals that call it home. Appeals to utilitarian purposes, while valuable, cannot ultimately succeed without a spiritual dimension that is centered on a deep reverence for life.[42]

Daniel Martin, a Roman Catholic missionary priest, writes that contemporary religion must find a way to "resanctify nature" and help people learn to "cherish" the earth.[43]

The same theme is expressed by the Russian author Fyodor Dostoyevski (1821–1881), who wrote that we should "love all creation, both the whole and every grain of sand":

> Love every leaf, every ray of light, all animals. If you love everything, you will perceive the mystery in all, and when you perceive this, you will grow every day in fuller understanding of it, until you come at last to love the whole world with a love that will be all-embracing and universal.[44]

The Right Reverend Vincent Rossi, director general of the Holy Order of MANS, a Christian brotherhood, believes that the solution to our environmental crisis is to rediscover and renew our instinctive awe for nature, which he calls a "living, sacred temple." His essay, "The Eleventh Commandment: Toward an Ethic of Ecology," argues that "the natural world must be seen as sacred because it is the abode of God":

> We must love nature for herself and also because she is a "handmaiden" of the lord. We must return to a kind of aboriginal consciousness of nature, an atonement for nature so direct one could not open the earth or cut down a tree or kill an animal without profound emotional response or a heartfelt prayer. Our awareness of nature must directly be

attached to our own feelings, as it once was for primitive man.

Nature is a theophany [the appearance or manifestation of the Deity]. Man must learn once again to see God everywhere in nature. We must let the scales fall from our eyes, and discerning the Divine presence in all things, love the earth and all nature as the visible Form of God.[45]

Carl Sagan, in the statement "Preserving and Cherishing the Earth," observed that "religious teaching, example, and leadership are powerfully able to influence personal conduct and commitment." Sagan wrote, "We understand that what is regarded as sacred is more likely to be treated with care and respect. Our planetary home should be so regarded. Efforts to safeguard and cherish the environment need to be infused with a vision of the sacred."[46]

Albert Schweitzer believed that a spiritual reverence for life was the essential attribute of a truly moral person. He wrote, "A man is ethical only when life, as such, is sacred to him, that of plants and animals as that of his fellow men, and when he devotes himself helpfully to all life that is in need of help."[47]

A FRAMEWORK FOR OUR OWN SOCIETY

The centuries-old traditions of philosophy, religion, and science, examined in this chapter, promote a reverence for life for all creatures. These traditions have been integral, if sometimes overlooked, parts of the religions of most cultures around the globe. Indeed, such a philosophy—old in wisdom and dating from remote periods—may be more practical and relevant today than ever. For at a time when the earth faces a potentially fatal ecological crisis, these principles provide us with a blueprint for preserving our planet and the life forms dependent on it. If properly understood and applied, they constitute a framework for building a truly humane society.

In such a society, we shall see that ordinary acts of kindness, consideration, respect, and reverence for animals can have extraordinary results. As change and instability accelerate in our new century, the humane ethic can be a mainstay for our own lives, for the natural world, and for civilization itself. As a guiding ethic that we can hold on to, believe in, and trust, it can give meaning to our lives and to the generations that follow.

OUR EARTHLY FAMILY

The ultimate irony of recognizing and accepting the intrinsic value of animals and nature and building a truly humane society is this: It is in our own selfish interest to do so. For protecting animals and their habitats would greatly benefit not only other creatures but human society as well, and may ultimately be essential to our own welfare and survival. HSUS Vice President Dr. John Grandy writes, "If we as a nation cannot preserve life for its own sake, then we ought to at least demand the preservation of endangered and threatened life forms for our own sake":

> The preservation of life on earth is inextricably tied to bio-logical diversity, that is, the diversity of life and genetic information that is contained in all of the species that inhabit this planet. This diversity of genetic information is continually renewed and revitalized through breeding and evolution. Extinction, which results in the permanent loss of genetic material and evolutionary potential, thus threat-ens the health of a wide diversity of ecosystems and the survival of all life.[48]

The Amazon Indians understand this all too well. The rain forests in which they live are being destroyed, depriving them of their home, their culture, their food supply, and their ability to continue to live as they have for millennia. But the rain forest is everyone else's habitat, too. It provides all of us with vital resources essential to our survival—oxygen, new drugs and medicines, and yet-to-be-discovered products we will never know we lost.

We are all dwellers in nature, aborigines of the earth, ultimately and totally dependent on one another and on the biological systems of the planet that we are so carelessly and rapidly damaging beyond repair. As Thomas Berry writes, "The various peoples of the Earth" are learning that "we have a common genetic line of development. Every living being of Earth is cousin to every other living being."[49]

A FAMILY TRAGEDY

As wilderness and wildlife habitat disappear, dooming so many creatures and species, we are experiencing a family tragedy. We should therefore not ask for whom the bell tolls, for it is truly tolling for us.

In *The Dream of the Earth*, distinguished author and historian Thomas Berry writes of the planet's "inherent powers in bringing forth [such a] marvelous display of beauty in such unending profusion, a display so overwhelming to human consciousness that we might very well speak of it as being dreamed into existence." Humans are an integral part of this fantastic pageant, and Dr. Berry emphasizes that "we must now understand that our own well-being can be achieved only through the well-being of the entire natural world about us."[50]

Jan Hartke of EarthVoice observes, "We share a physical, evolutionary, and spiritual kinship with all creation":

> This reality gives us the innate capacity to empathize with all of earth's life forms, to touch the deepest chords of our being, and feel a part of the vast, subtle, mysterious connections and interdependence that we have with all the earth's life forms, animate and inanimate alike. Empathy, the capacity to see through the eyes of other creatures, changes everything. Empathy has a certain magical quality; it is the precondition to caring. Seeing through the eyes of another creature or being makes everything flow automatically—compassion, justice, respect, reverence, and love.[51]

Thus, in order to "save the planet" and build a truly humane society, we will have to change our attitudes towards the planet and its nonhuman inhabitants. In a speech to The World Council of Churches, theologian Charles Birch noted, "All creatures are fellow creatures, and human responsibility extends infinitely to the whole of creation . . . if we are to continue to inhabit the earth, there has to be a revolution in the relationship of human beings to the earth, and . . . to each other."[52]

We must relearn the ancient and immutable laws of ecology understood so well by our forebears, by our spiritual elders, and by those still living in and close to nature. Thus, we do not have to adopt new religious, philosophical, and scientific principles. We merely have to return to the roots of our old ones.

A DREAM OF THE EARTH

In *The Universe Story*, Thomas Berry eloquently recounts the 15 billion-year history of the cosmos, and the 4 billion-year history of life on earth. He warns that "we are now experiencing that exciting moment when our new meaning, our new story is taking shape":

> The present disintegration of the life systems of the Earth is so extensive that we might very well be bringing an end to the Cenozoic period that has provided the identity for the life processes of earth during the past sixty-seven million years. During this period, life expanded with amazing fluorescence prior to the coming of the human.[53]

But now, Dr. Berry notes, humans have radically changed the equation:

> The human has taken over such extensive control of the life systems of the Earth that the future will be dependent on human decision to an extent never dreamed of in previous times. We are deciding what species will live or perish, we are determining the chemical structure of the soil and the air and the water, we are mapping out the areas of wilderness that will be allowed to function in their own natural modalities.[54]

It has been given to us to write a new chapter in the story of the universe—to imagine a new earth. Because of our ever-expanding numbers and technology, we have attained the power, for the first time in human history, to destroy the beauty, diversity, and natural functioning of the life forms of our planet. Indeed, we are well on our way towards accomplishing this.

Will we recognize in time that the exercise of unbridled power without compassion or foresight is a formula for disaster? Can we succeed in building a humane society early enough in the new millennium to forestall disaster, and to create a pervasive spirit of kindness and gentleness that will settle over the land and all of the creatures of creation? These are the critical questions of our time.

In building our new society, we will need a broad coalition from all segments of society. For support and guidance, we must look to religion and ethics, philosophy and science. But we must also look to government and business, poets and musicians, dreamers and prophets, shamans and visionaries. We must seek to inspire and cooperate with people from all walks of life who can comprehend the necessity for a central humane principle that conveys the spirit of reverence, restraint, and renewal.

This unifying principle gives us the opportunity—our last and only chance, perhaps—to meaningfully address the globally interlocking problems that threaten our future. The odds of our succeeding may not seem encouraging, but, as anthropologist Margaret Mead has counseled, "Never doubt that a small group of people can change the world; indeed, it is the only thing that has ever done so."

So let us dare to dream. Let us, together, dream of a day when the disastrous practices that ravage the earth and its creatures become things of the past and are ended forever. Let us hope that when people look back at the end of the next century or the next millennium, they can say that we are the generation that changed the course of history, that planted the seeds for a sustainable and humane society, and that gave The Universe Story a happy ending after all.

PART II

The Threat to Our Civilization

2. ARE WE KILLING OUR PLANET?

For the first time in a thousand years, we have the opportunity to begin a new millennium with the knowledge, the ability, and, most of all, the determination to set a course for the future that will ensure security and prosperity for those who follow in our steps. The choice is ours. We can begin the long journey towards sustaining and protecting our civilization, or we can continue down the much shorter road to disaster. We can begin to solve our environmental problems, or we can bring on "an unending series of disasters."[1]

If we are to learn from our mistakes and work to correct them, the new millennium must bring with it new ways of thinking about and acting towards the earth's inhabitants and biological systems, including our fellow creatures and their natural habitats. If we can begin to understand that our fate and theirs are intertwined, we can enter a new era that will bring with it a secure and sustainable future for all of the earth's inhabitants. But if our old ways of thinking and acting persist, I fear for the future of our wildlife, of our planet, and of human civilization itself.

IS IT THE END OF THE WORLD?

The end of one millennium and the start of a new one has traditionally been a time of apocalyptic visions and prophecies of doomsday—of foretelling the end of the world. As we begin our new millennium, we must rationally wonder if this time the world really *may* be coming to an end—or, at least, if so much of it will be destroyed that our society will be profoundly changed for the worse, with much of its beauty, diversity, and value gone forever.

While this and much of what follows in this book may sound overly alarmist, it is based on or supported by the best available scientific data. No longer can any of us plead ignorance. The point of no return is approaching rapidly, and decisions must now be made that will determine the fate of the planet.

There is today more discussion and reporting of environmental problems than ever before, and the public has become increasingly concerned about the impact of these threats. But people generally are not aware that while progress is being made on some issues, *none* of the major problems is being adequately addressed, and *all* are getting worse.

On November 18, 1992, "The World Scientists' Warning to Humanity" was issued, starkly describing the grave threat to our planet's future:

> We hereby warn all humanity of what lies ahead. A great change in our stewardship of the earth and the life on it, is required if vast human misery is to be avoided, and our global home on this planet is not to be irretrievably mutilated.[2]

The statement went on to observe that "much of the damage is irreversible on a scale of centuries, or permanent. . . . If not checked, many of our current practices put at serious risk the future that we wish for human society and for the plant and animal kingdoms, and may so alter the living world that it will be unable to sustain life in the manner that we know."[3]

The warning was signed by 1,575 of the world's top scientists from 69 countries, including 99 Nobel Prize winners in the sciences. It represented "the largest group of senior scientists from around the world ever to speak in unison on a single issue," as one participant put it.

But it should hardly come as a surprise that our planet is in deep trouble. A casual reading of the daily newspapers, or a careful study of the most authoritative scientific data available, compel the same conclusion. The ongoing human destruction of the natural environment is damaging—permanently, irreversibly, and perhaps fatally—the earth's ability to recover, to heal itself, and to continue to support those biological processes that have sustained life on earth for hundreds of millions of years. Today, there are about a dozen categories of critical environmental problems we face, any *one* of which could be devastating to our society.

Our current economic, energy, and agricultural policies are simply not sustainable over the long haul. Yet almost every nation continues to follow the same basic developmental strategies adopted at the beginning of the industrial revolution two centuries ago, and pursued with particular zeal in the half century since the end of World War II.[4] Indeed, human activity has done more damage to the planet in the last fifty years than in all of the rest of recorded history. And if we continue these policies into the new millennium, we will destroy enough of the remaining ecological and agricultural systems on which we all depend to place our future in jeopardy. Even if we modify our policies and reduce their destructiveness, present trends will continue at a slower pace, eroding the underpinnings of our society—especially the food production systems—and bringing about the end of civilization as we know it.

THE THREATS OF OVERPOPULATION AND POVERTY

Perhaps our biggest problem is the one that contributes to and exacerbates all of the others: Human overpopulation. There are already too many humans on earth for the available resources, and many more humans are on the way. In fact, over 200,000 people are added every day, for a yearly net increase—births minus deaths—of some 78 million. During the first dozen years or so of the new millennium, we will add a billion more people to our already overcrowded world of 6 billion—a point that was reached in October 1999. And the 6-billion mark itself is over *double* the global population at mid-century, and more than four times what it was at the beginning of that century.[5]

We do not have to wait to observe the disastrous impact of too many humans consuming too few resources. For much of the world, the environmental crisis has already arrived. Largely as a result of the destitution caused by natural resource shortages and overcrowding in the Third World, a quarter of the world's people live in such utter poverty—on less than one dollar a day—that one can hardly conceive how they manage to survive.

But while one end of lifeboat earth is sinking, those of us at the other end can hardly look on complacently or try to avert our gaze. We cannot ignore the fact that so many of our fellow humans endure lives of total desperation, hopelessly trapped in destitution, misery, and hunger. One in three of the world's children is undernourished. And *every day*, some 40,000 to 50,000 children die of hunger, disease, and malnutrition.[6]

It is difficult for those of us in the industrialized world—we who enjoy the greatest age of abundance and wealth the world has ever seen—to have any idea of the poverty and deprivation that characterize the lives of much of humanity. But it is clear that we cannot attain a humane and sustainable society without improving the lot of the poor. Consider the following statistics:

❏ Of the 6 billion people on earth as of October 1999, 1.5 billion are living on one dollar a day or less. This indicates an increase of 200 million abjectly poor people just since 1993. Over a billion more people survive on less than two dollars a day.[7]

❏ The combined gross domestic products (GDPs) of the world's forty-eight poorest nations is lower than the combined assets of the world's three richest people.[8]

In its "Human Development Report—1998," the United Nations Development Program (UNDP) states:

> Of the 4.4 billion people in developing countries, nearly three-fifths lack basic sanitation. Almost a third have no access to clean water. A quarter do not have adequate housing. A fifth have no access to modern health services. A fifth of children do not attend school to grade 5. . . . Worldwide, two billion people are anemic. . . .[9]

The huge disparities in wealth and consumption between the rich nations and the poor ones have resulted in a small number of countries' causing most of the pollution, environmental destruction, and depletion of natural resources. Think about the following:

❏ Americans consume 250 times more energy per capita than people in poor nations.[10]

❏ The city of Chicago and its 3 million people consume as much as a southeast Asian nation of 97 million.[11]

❏ The world's wealthiest nations, constituting 20 percent of the world's population, account for 86 percent of all private expenditures for consumption. The poorest 20 percent spend only 1.3 percent.[12]

❏ Americans spend more money every year on cosmetics ($8 billion), and Europeans spend more on ice cream ($11 billion), than it would cost to provide sanitation and water ($9 billion) or basic education ($6 billion) to the world's 2 billion people who, as of 1998, lacked schools and toilets.[13, 14]

CATASTROPHIC CLIMATE CHANGES

Our modern civilization could be completely disrupted by the change in climate and weather that is being created largely by chemical and industrial pollution. The two major problems are the destruction of the upper atmosphere's protective ozone layer and global warming—the so-called greenhouse effect. These problems continue to worsen year after year, despite international agreements aimed at mitigating them in the years ahead.

Each of the first five months of 1998 set global temperature records. It was easily the warmest year on record, and part of the warmest decade ever. With higher temperatures comes more energy to charge and churn the planet's climate, producing more intense storms, greater flooding, and more general destruction. Droughts, fires, and crop failures are also exacerbated by the increased energy, heat, and violent weather caused by global warming.[15]

We are already seeing a sample of the destructive potential of climate change. In 1998, weather-related "natural" disasters killed over 41,000 people, rendered 300 million people homeless, and caused some $92 billion in damages. These costs exceeded by over 50 percent the previous record of $60 billion in economic losses incurred in 1996, and topped total damages during the entire decade of the 1980s![16]

The Increase of Weather-Related Disasters

Some of the notable weather-related catastrophes of 1998 were greatly exacerbated by earlier large-scale deforestation and the removal of trees that had absorbed rainfall and held soil in place. As a result, heavy rainfall on bare hillsides washed away the soil—along with the villages and people living on and below them. The results of this were truly horrifying:

❏ In China, the flooding of the Yangtze River made 56 million people homeless, drowned 3,656 people, and caused $36 billion in damages.[17]

❏ In Bangladesh, monsoons flooded two-thirds of the country for over a month, displacing 21 million people. There and in India, monsoons killed 4,500 people, caused 55 million people to lose their homes, and resulted in $5 billion in losses. [18]

❏ In Honduras, Hurricane Mitch, the worst Atlantic storm in 200 years, washed away dozens of villages, leaving a third of the population homeless; killing over 11,000; and ruining 70 percent of the crops. As Honduran president Flores put it, in several days, the hurricane destroyed "what it took 50 years to build."[19]

❏ Record heat waves swept through many countries, killing 3,000 in India and 100 in Texas.[20]

The next year—1999—also had its share of unprecedented, extraordinarily violent weather. A heat wave in the northeastern United States killed over 270 people. In September, Hurricane Floyd devastated eastern North Carolina, leaving over $1 billion in damages in its wake. In November, 10,000 people in eastern India died in a massive cyclone. In December, Venezuela experienced its worst natural disaster in modern times, when rains of Biblical proportions caused flooding and mudslides that killed upwards of 15,000 people.[21]

The year ended with fiercely violent windstorms in Western Europe, where winds gusted up to 125 miles per hour, causing over $4 billion in losses and killing more than 100 people. Some 60,000 trees in two forests outside Paris were uprooted and toppled, as were 10,000 trees at the royal palace at Versailles, including 200-year-old cedars planted during the French Revolution. By some estimates, the storms destroyed the equivalent of 1,250,000 acres of woodlands. French forestry officials said that some 270 million trees were uprooted or broken in half. They further stated that it would take up to two centuries for France's forests to recover.[22, 23, 24]

There is growing evidence that global warming may be feeding on itself, increasing the intensity and frequency of tropical storms and other extreme weather. Hurricanes and other storms produce intense wind speed that may so stir the ocean that greater amounts of heat-trapping carbon dioxide are released. This, in turn, releases more energy into the atmosphere, greatly exacerbating global warming and the storms that are produced as a result.[25, 26]

Ultimately, the destruction that is taking place today may pale in comparison with the damage that could occur in future years. As the polar ice caps melt and ocean levels rise, low-lying islands and coastal areas will be inundated, displacing tens, perhaps hundreds, of millions of people. Regions expected to be most affected by rising sea levels are much of the East and West Coasts of the United States, including New York City, Boston, Los Angeles, and San Francisco; and large areas of North and South Carolina, Georgia, and Florida. Louisiana, too, will be affected.[27, 28]

As water levels rise, entire island states—the Seychelles, the Maldives, Micronesia, and the Gilbert and Marshall Islands, for instance—may disappear under water. In June 1999, experts at the South Pacific Regional Environment Program reported that two uninhabited islands in the area, Tebua Tarawa and Abanuea, had recently disappeared because of rising sea levels. Other islands belonging to Kiribati and Tuvalu were in danger of being submerged, with valuable cropland and ancestral burial grounds already inundated.[29] That same month, the Pew Center on Climate Change warned that the new millennium would begin with an acceleration of the global warming trend, with the first 100 years experiencing the same degree of temperature rises—7 percent—that occurred during the last 20,000 years. [30]

In December 1999, government scientists reported that in the mid-1970s, average global surface temperatures had begun increasing at a rate of 3.5 degrees Fahrenheit per century, and would continue to rise by 2 to 6 degrees over the next 100 years. While this rate may appear moderate, it is astoundingly rapid given that since the depths of the last ice age, 18,000 to 20,000 years ago, the world has warmed by only 5 to 9 degrees.[31]

The nineties were the warmest decade on record, and probably the hottest in thousands of years. Ross Gelbspan, author of *The*

Heat Is On, warns, "These signs of atmospheric warming are omens of a much larger disruption that is coming at us very quickly," and "threaten to disrupt and alter permanently a relatively stable and coherent civilization":

> With the surge in our oil and coal burning, we have set in motion massive systems of the planet—systems with huge amounts of inertia that have kept them relatively hospitable for the last 10,000 years. We have loosed a wave of violent and chaotic weather. We have altered the timing of the seasons. We are living on a precarious outcropping of stability.[32]

Ozone Layer Depletion

The stratospheric ozone layer helps make life on earth possible by shielding it from 95 to 99 percent of the deadly ultraviolet radiation from the sun. Without this radiation shield, life on our planet would not have survived and evolved. The thinning of the ozone layer jeopardizes our continued existence.

The sun's radiation does not only kill wildlife, crops, and vegetation, but also causes cataracts, weakened immune systems, and fatal skin cancers in humans. Since the mid-1970s, we have known that the ozone layer is being broken apart by industrial chemicals such as chloroflourocarbons (CFCs), and pesticides such as methyl bromide and carbon tetrachloride.[33, 34, 35]

The most obvious manifestation of the thinning ozone layer occurs every year over the North and South Poles, where massive "holes" appear every winter and spring. In October 1998, government scientists at NASA and the National Oceanic and Atmospheric Administration (NOAA) announced that the ozone hole over Antarctica had grown larger than North America. Moreover, measuring 10 million square miles, it was the biggest ozone hole ever observed.[36]

One result of the thinning ozone layer has been a dramatic increase in the incidence of skin cancers, with malignant melanoma, once a rare disorder, becoming the world's fastest-rising type of cancer. In 1999, over a million Americans were diagnosed with nonfatal skin cancers.[37]

Most of the industrialized nations have agreed to phase out the production and use of CFCs and other ozone-destroying chemicals. But in the meantime, these chemicals continue to wreak havoc. The United States has placed major restrictions on CFCs, but the pesticide methyl bromide remains in widespread use. It was scheduled to be largely banned in the year 2001, but in 1998, Congress and the Clinton-Gore Administration extended its use to 2005.[38, 39]

Unfortunately, the depletion of the ozone layer will continue for decades after the major problem chemicals are banned. It takes six to eight years for some of the compounds to reach the upper atmosphere, where they can remain active for up to twenty-five years. Thus, even if production of all such chemicals were halted—a highly unlikely event—the compounds already released would continue to destroy ozone for at least another quarter of a century. As former Senator George Mitchell observed after holding hearings on the issue, these chemicals "threaten the very ability of the planet earth to support life as we know it."[40]

UNDERMINING SOCIETY'S FOUNDATIONS

Other critical environmental problems we face include the virtually permanent loss or severe depletion of our groundwater, wetlands, fisheries, and topsoil from croplands—the latter at a rate of 2 to 3 billion tons a year in the United States, and 25 billion tons worldwide.

In India, which adds 18 million people a year to its population of almost a billion, the ongoing depletion of the nation's groundwater could reduce the grain harvest by up to 25 percent. Even in America, cropland is disappearing. Every day, 7,000 acres of farmland and open space are lost to development. These trends, which prevail across the globe, will mean far less food production potential in future years for the rapidly growing human population.[41, 42]

The massive destruction of wildlife and wilderness, especially old-growth and tropical rain forests, is denuding our planet of much of its beauty, biological diversity, climate stability, and sources of oxygen production and carbon dioxide absorption.

Tropical forests are being cut at a rate of one or two acres a second, clearing an area the size of Washington State or Finland every year. This deforestation is thought to be wiping out several species of birds, animals, and plants every hour. Many of the plant species being destroyed could be extremely important as future sources of drugs, medicines, and food. So we could be regularly losing possible cures for cancer and other dread diseases, as well as food sources potentially as important as rice, corn, and wheat.[43]

PRICING THE PLANET

It is nearly impossible to quantify or place a monetary value on the earth's natural biological systems, since they are literally priceless and absolutely essential to our welfare and survival. But in May 1997, thirteen economists, ecologists, and other scientists published "The Value of the World's Ecosystem Services and Natural Capital." These experts placed a price tag of up to $54 trillion per year on the worth of the biosphere.

> The services of ecological systems and the natural capital stocks that produce them are critical to the functioning of the Earth's life-support system. They contribute to human welfare . . . and therefore represent part of the total economic value of the planet. We have estimated the current economic value of 17 ecosystem services . . . to be in the range of $16 to $54 trillion per year, with an average of $33 trillion.[44]

It is interesting to note that the estimated average worth of $33 trillion is almost double the global gross national product (GNP) of $18 trillion. The report characterized its figures as "a minimum estimate," adding that "the real value is almost certainly much larger." It warned that giving the data "too little weight in policy decisions . . . may ultimately compromise the sustainability of humans in the biosphere. . . . The economies of the earth would grind to a halt without the services of ecological life-support systems," the scientists concluded, "so in one sense their total value to the economy is infinite."[45]

EARTH ISLAND

There are historical precedents for our wasteful squandering of natural resources. The mysterious disappearance of the inhabitants of Easter Island several hundred years ago holds important lessons for our society on the value and, indeed, the necessity of conservation.

Located in the South Pacific, 1,900 miles west of South America, the forty-five-square-mile island was settled by Polynesians 1,500 years ago. By the sixteenth century, a sophisticated agricultural society was thriving there.

But when Europeans discovered the island in the seventeenth century, they were greeted only by huge stone statues built by the Polynesians. Their mute testimony provided tragic evidence of the demise of a society. The humans were all gone, their civilization having collapsed within the span of a few decades.

The islanders apparently perished because they had used up their natural resources, much as we are doing today. In the words of Lester Brown and Christopher Flavin of the Worldwatch Institute, "The demise of this society was triggered by the decimation of its limited resource base . . . its own resources ran out."[46]

As the human population expanded, the lush forest was cut to clear land for growing crops and to provide fuel and tree trunks as rollers to haul the huge statues across the island. The loss of trees removed the source of home- and boat-building materials, and caused massive soil erosion. Since fish and crops could no longer be obtained, a drastic reduction in the food supply eventually led to starvation, cannibalism, and warfare.

As Brown and Flavin point out, "Easter Island presents a particularly stark picture of what can happen when a human economy expands in the face of limited resources. . . . The human race as a whole has reached the kind of turning point that the Easter Islanders reached in the sixteenth century."[47]

What happened at Easter Island was long ago and far away. But if we ignore its implications for our own society, we place ourselves at great risk.

POISONING OUR SOCIETY

In many ways, these are the best of times for the human race. In the middle of the eighteenth century in London, average life expectancy was twenty-five years of age—about what it was in ancient Rome. Today, global life expectancy has risen to an all-time high of sixty-six years, and in the industrial world, it is seventy-five.[48]

Americans commonly live into their eighties. There are 50,000 centenarians—people of a hundred or more years of age—in the country now. At the turn of the century, there were almost none.[49]

We live in an unprecedented era of abundance. As John Tuxill of the Worldwatch Institute observes, "Society now grows more food than ever before, and those who can purchase it have a material standard of living unimaginable to earlier generations."[50] We are so incredibly wealthy that we can afford to throw away 96 billion pounds of food each year, an amount that could easily feed all of the nation's hungry people.[51]

But we must not become complacent about the remarkable progress we have made. We must ensure that we did not come all this way to see our human progress rapidly swept away in a flood of pollution, climate change, food shortages, and epidemics.

About half of all Americans today die prematurely of heart disease, a disorder caused or exacerbated in large part by our high-fat, meat-centered diet. Raising cattle and other animals to satisfy our demand for meat may cause more pollution and resource depletion than all other human activities combined. Livestock occupy and destructively graze on perhaps half the useable land mass of the earth, often damaging it severely.

Cancer strikes almost 1 American in 3—at a rate of over 3,000 people a day—and kills some 565,000 every year. Of the 270 million Americans now alive, over 80 million can expect to develop cancer in their lifetimes.[52]

More Americans die of cancer every year than were killed in combat in World War II, Korea, and Vietnam combined. Cancer has become more common among the young as well as the old, with the incidence of childhood cancers, especially leukemia and brain tumors, mounting sharply in recent years.

Much of this cancer epidemic is the result of cigarette smoking, but some appears to be the result of the pervasive contamination of our environment and food chain with deadly pesticides and toxic chemicals. With our constant, unavoidable, life-long exposure to cancer-causing chemicals, a disease once considered rare now strikes 1.2 million Americans a year, not counting a million usually nonfatal skin cancers.

Additional deadly diseases are on the way. As Dr. Paul Epstein of the Harvard Medical School points out, "Global warming may have grave consequences for future control of disease." He continues, "The current world-wide warming trend is likely to increase the exposure of millions of people to new diseases and health risks. . . . At least 30 new infectious diseases have emerged in the past 20 years."[53]

Some of the newly emerged diseases in the United States include hantavirus pulmonary syndrome and Lyme disease. Worldwide, close to 300 million people suffer from malaria, and 1 to 2 million die from it every year. As the globe heats up, a million more deaths from malaria could begin occurring annually, and the number of people at risk of contracting the disease could increase from 42 percent of the world's population to 60 percent. Although the United States has largely escaped the malaria scourge, outbreaks occurred in the early 1990s during hot, humid periods in New York and New Jersey. Such outbreaks could become much worse in coming years."[54]

THE ROOTS OF OUR CRISIS

How did we get into such a mess, and how do we get out? One of the biggest mistakes made was our failure to heed the early apparent consequences of our environmental problems. These consequences included bird and fish kills by pesticides and pollution; the endangerment of such faraway species as tigers and elephants; the disappearance of the vast summer swarms of butterflies and fireflies in many areas, and of the frogs and toads that filled our creeks and ponds; and the destruction of forests and wilderness, of neighborhood woods and wildlife.

Many of us felt that we could ignore these events with impunity, since our personal lives seemed affected little, if at all. Thus, we remained calm and complacent. Even when the evidence of crisis began to mount, we refused to act. We came to accept the pollution of our air and water, the pesticide contamination of our food, and the presence of toxic substances virtually everywhere.

Perhaps if we had been more humane, more concerned about the plight of our fellow creatures, we could have avoided the crisis we now face. But now, with critical environmental threats coming at us from all sides, it is difficult for even the most shortsighted to avoid the realization that we are running out of options—and that the stakes have risen dramatically.

Today, it is not just snail darters and seals, eagles and elephants that are threatened. It is the earth itself and those life forms living and dependent on the planet, including humans.

It is late in the game, and as Thomas Berry has observed, our environmental problems hold the *potential* for extinguishing much of the life on the planet, and the *certainty* of drastically degrading its quality.[55]

WHAT CAN BE DONE?

Given all of these dangers and disasters, it is difficult to be optimistic about our chances of "saving the planet," its natural environment and wildlife, and the biological systems indispensable to our own survival. But if it is hard for us to be very hopeful, it is impossible for us to abandon hope, for that would ensure the defeat of the efforts of so many to perpetuate human society and the natural mechanisms that have for eons sustained it.

If we make the wrong decisions in the years immediately ahead, there will be no turning back. Our generation of humans is the last one fortunate enough to have the resources, the opportunities, and the options that are available to us today. Never again will a generation of humans have a mission so awesome as the one given to us—to take a world teetering on disaster, and make it safe and healthy again.

This is our last chance on earth. We must not fail in this task.

3. THE DEMISE OF
AMERICAN AGRICULTURE

There is no activity more important to our society—and to other societies across the globe—than agriculture. Gary L. Valen, Director of Sustainable Agriculture for The HSUS, writes, "Agriculture is an ancient relationship between humans and nature that provides sustenance and livelihood for all the generations we call civilization." He continues, "The foundations of human organizations, from family units to empires, are based on the ability to produce food."[1]

And agriculture affects even more than our food supply and our human organizations. Dean Freudenberger of Luther Seminary in Roseville, Minnesota, once wrote, "In this modern world, the way agriculture is done will very much determine the destiny of the planet."[2] Regrettably, our agricultural policy bodes trouble for our planet. As Kentucky farmer Wendell Berry said, "Our farm policy, like our energy policy, is simply to use up all we have."[3] Today, we are rapidly and radically transforming farming into an industrial enterprise that is causing drastic dislocations and changes in our society. Before we go much farther down this road, we should be sure that we understand where we are going, and decide whether we really want to proceed past the point of no return into this frightening world of "the new agriculture."

45

GOODBYE TO THE FAMILY FARM

Some of my best memories of childhood are of visiting my grand-parents' family farm and seeing happy, free-roaming animals and their proud owners, all enjoying their connection to one another and to the land.

But things have changed drastically in recent years, as I was shocked to see in a visit to Milford, Utah. A few years ago, several of us inspected an industrial hog-raising operation—from the road, since tight security keeps out anyone not authorized to enter. What we encountered was shocking, especially since it may represent the future of American agriculture.

We saw mile after mile of "farm buildings" scattered over an almost empty landscape, housing over a million pigs. Strangely, we saw almost no animals or humans of any kind, much less "farmers." It was an odd and eerie landscape, seemingly deserted, but crammed full of hidden and suffering animals, crowded together in conditions of almost unbelievable squalor. With wind conditions right, you could smell the stench twenty miles away.

Traveling some fifty miles over this wasteland, we saw only about fifteen humans, and the only activity we observed was that of huge trucks hauling away the hogs. Before construction, the facility had been presented to the local community as an economically sustainable business that would provide employment, revitalization, and other benefits to the area. But all the factory farm really brought were huge, jail-like buildings, massive amounts of hog manure, and the suffering of hundreds of thousands of sentient animals.

It was obvious to anyone that this was not farming, that these were not farmers, and that the "production units " they were raising were being treated more like machines than animals.

FACTORY FARMS

The factory farm we observed in Utah is a joint venture of the four largest pork producers in the United States. And, unfortunately, it is rather typical of what is becoming the dominant type of "farming" in this country—not just in the raising of hogs, but in the raising of most livestock.

Hog Farming

At the time we visited the Utah farm, the facility had about 1.5 million hogs "under production," and was reportedly producing almost the same amount of waste as the state's entire population of 2 million people. The operation's goal for the end of the decade was to increase production to 2.5 million hogs—all of whom would be crowded together in a twenty-five-mile stretch of buildings.[4]

Only a very small percentage of the manure produced at such hog farms can be absorbed by the land, so open lagoons of waste matter—each the size of one or several football fields—have to be built. These lagoons inevitably attract hordes of flies and produce nauseating odors and noxious gases such as ammonia, hydrogen sulfide, and methane, the latter being a contributing cause of global warming and ozone layer depletion.[5]

Pigs are intelligent and social animals, but in such facilities they are denied their most basic physical and social needs. Up to 12,000 pigs are often crammed into a single, enclosed building that is longer than a football field. There, they spend their entire lives. The females (sows) are usually stuffed into tiny crates so small they cannot turn around, much less walk. They are forced to give birth and nurse their young in the same small, filthy space where they defecate—something any mother mammal would find repulsive. [6, 7, 8]

These are the conditions under which farms raise about 90 percent of the over 100 million hogs slaughtered each year in the United States. And more and more hog farms are turning to these "confinement conditions." The number of small and independent pig farms has dropped by some 75 percent over the last fifteen years, and four major corporations now control more than half of all hog-slaughtering operations.[9, 10, 11]

The Farming of Other Livestock

Miserable conditions, similar to those at hog-raising facilities, prevail for most of the over 8 billion food animals killed every year in the United States. This includes a *daily* toll of over 7,000 calves, 130,000 cattle, 360,000 pigs, 900,000 turkeys, 70,000 ducks, and an astonishing 24 million chickens. (Worldwide, an estimated 43 billion animals were killed for food in 1998.)[12, 13, 14]

A typical factory farm can raise up to two million chickens at one site, crowding 20,000 to 30,000 "broiler" chickens or 100,000 egg-laying hens in each building. The birds are crammed into battery cages so small that the chickens cannot even spread their wings. Veal calves spend their lives in cages so narrow they cannot turn around, thus keeping the meat tender and lacking muscle. They are deliberately denied proper nourishment in order to produce the pale color so valued by consumers, and are fed artificial hormones and antibiotics to accelerate their growth and prevent disease.[15, 16, 17]

Beef cattle are the least restricted of farm animals, but are usually given no shade or shelter on feedlots. Dairy cows are typically tied in stalls or housed in metal stocks called stanchions, which permit no movement except standing or lying down.[18]

While many would consider such conditions abominable, they are actually desirable from the viewpoint of the producer, since they allow the largest number of animals to be grown in the smallest possible space at the lowest cost, thus maximizing productivity and profits. But, as the report "Creating a New Vision of Farming" observes, this new—and now dominant—form of agriculture "generates great wealth from the countryside, and returns poverty and dispossession to farmers and workers, harm to nature, depopulation and disintegration of its communities, churches, and civic organizations. It is industrial agriculture. Without our concerted thought and action, it is the future."[19, 20]

THE HUMAN VICTIMS

The industrializing of American agriculture not only makes life miserable for billions of animals, but also is dooming family farmers and the rural communities that support them. Further, factory farms adversely affect the health of both the farmers who work in them and the consumers who use the resulting products.

Dwindling Farm Communities

It is a sad fact that factory farms are depriving young people of the opportunity to adopt the still-proud profession of farming as a livelihood. As Wendell Berry laments, "We have lost farmers in staggering numbers, mainly because of economic adversity. For generations, we have given nothing to farm-raised children but reasons to leave home. Our farm communities have disintegrated everywhere." [21]

Indeed, during the twentieth century, rural America has experienced a drastic loss of population, and factory farms have accelerated this trend. Between 1940 and 1985, the farm population declined by over 80 percent, from 30 million to 5.4 million. In the period between 1985 and 1990, over 425,000 family farms went out of business, and a few large agribusiness corporations took their places. In fact, over a fifth of America's pork supply is now slaughtered by *one* company, Smithfield Foods, and four large companies do 70 percent of all cattle slaughtering. [22] As the pace of mechanization has accelerated in recent years, petroleum-based fuel, fertilizer, and pesticides have replaced the labor formerly provided by humans and animals. Farmers now constitute less than 2 percent of the population, and less than 6 percent of current farmers are under age thirty-four. Clearly, farming as we know it—real farming—is dying out. [23, 24, 25]

Many of the surviving farmers have found it difficult to remain independent, and have been forced to raise crops and/or animals for giant agribusiness corporations in order to stay in business. Even Agriculture Secretary Dan Glickman warned, "There's a fear this will turn into fourteenth century feudalism. Those farmers will become serfs. We're not here yet, but it may be coming." [26]

Richard Clugston, director of the Center for Respect of Life and Environment (CRLE), points out that the result of this trend is increasing rural unemployment and poverty, degradation of the land and the environment, and "loss of a sense of place and culture":

> Farmers and small town dwellers are displaced, but since decent or adequate jobs do not exist either in the big cities or regional centers, they become welfare dependent. . . . Petroleum intensive, monoculture-based, mechanized agriculture continues to deplete and degrade the environment. Soil erodes, water is used up, crops and animals are more subject to disease and stress. Environmental damage increases. Both the quantity and quality of food and fiber drops. [27]

This rapid industrialization of our agriculture, Dr. Clugston notes, will ultimately have dire consequences for our children and grandchildren:

[This] will result in the deterioration of the quality of life for current rural (and increasingly all global) citizens, because it depletes, erodes, and pollutes the land and environment, and undermines cultural and biological richness and diversity; and its true cost will be paid primarily by future generations.[28]

The Threat to Factory Farmers

The factory operations that are replacing family farms not only employ few people, but also offer working conditions that are dangerous and unhealthy. Because the regulations of the Occupational Safety and Health Administration (OSHA) do not, for the most part, cover factory farms, workers are often exposed to hazardous levels of carbon monoxide and other toxic gases, to microbes, and to harmful airborne particles. Serious health problems have affected up to 90 percent of workers in pig-confinement buildings. In Ohio, an "intensive confinement" operation raising hens in battery cages was reported to be emitting, through 700 unfiltered fans, a *daily* blizzard of some 2,500 pounds of dust, chicken feathers, skin particles, and manure.[29]

Conditions are particularly gruesome in poultry plants, where some workers handle 15,000 chicken parts a day. These workers "wear out" from the constant repetitive motion involved in the assembly line work. Chicken "catchers" round up as many as 25,000 chickens in a day. Some 40,000 workers are injured every year in the industry, resulting in many later being dismissed for "poor worker performance."[30]

People who live in the vicinity of factory farms, particularly downwind, are known to suffer from a myriad of psychological and physical problems, including nausea, depression, frequent vomiting, and respiratory difficulties. They also suffer economically from lowered property values and the degeneration of their neighborhoods.[31]

The Threat to Consumers

By crowding farm animals together and routinely feeding them drugs, modern farm practices have rendered meat products from such animals unsafe by increasing the incidence of contamination with such deadly compounds as *Salmonella*, which causes 1.4 million illnesses a year and kills 550 people; *Campylobacter*, which infects 4 million people a year, killing 200 to 1,000; and antibiotic-resistant bacteria. The deadly *E. coli* bacteria is found on about a quarter of the nation's ground beef and causes 110,000 illnesses a year, some of which have been fatal to children.[32, 33, 34, 35]

No one knows how many people are sickened or killed by contaminated meat and dairy products, since many food poisoning cases are attributed to flu or other illness. But the United States Centers for Disease Control (CDC) estimates that, each year in the United States, food-borne pathogens—which come mainly from animal products—cause 76 million illnesses, 325,000 hospitalizations, and 5,000 deaths. For every American, every year, the odds of becoming sick from contaminated food are one in four.[36]

At the same time, efforts by factory farms to prevent disease outbreaks from decimating their overcrowded animals and to speed their animals' growth are threatening to undermine one of the greatest achievements of modern medicine. By feeding the animals massive amounts of antibiotics, these operations are destroying the effectiveness of these medicines and rendering them useless in fighting human infections.

In the United States, 40 percent of the 50 million pounds of antibiotics annually produced are fed to farm animals, mainly as feed additives. The result has been an increase in infections in people, some fatal, involving bacteria that are drug-resistant, and so cannot be treated with antibiotics.[37, 38]

A CDC study of food samples from around the country found that the prevalence of a strain of *Salmonella* that had become resistant to five types of antibiotics increased from 0.6 percent in 1980 to 34 percent in 1996. And the incidence of drug-resistant *Campylobacter* bacteria had risen from zero in 1991 to 14 percent in 1998. When Minnesota's health department sampled chickens in supermarkets, it found that 88 percent carried strains of *Campylobacter*, 20 percent of which were drug-resistant.[39]

Dr. Fred Angulo, a medical epidemiologist at the CDC, warns that there is consensus within the scientific community that increasing levels of drug-resistant bacteria are being caused by the use of antibiotics in livestock. According to Angulo, "Public health is united in the conclusion; there is no controversy about where antibiotic resistance in food-borne pathogens comes from."[40]

The deliberate, continued use of such drugs by factory farmers is blunting one of our most potent weapons against disease and endangering the public's health. Abandoning the widespread use of antibiotics in livestock would make intense confinement a much less profitable way to raise animals, but it might prevent a public health disaster and save the lives of many Americans.

Risking Our Children's Health

The fact is that even uncontaminated, factory farm-raised food threatens the public's health, particularly that of children. The intensive, extremely efficient methods used to produce high volumes of meat, eggs, and dairy products, combined with huge government subsidies, allow the industry to sell such products at artificially low prices. The affordability of these high-fat and high-cholesterol foods encourages people to use such potentially unhealthy products as dietary staples—in many cases, as the center of their diets.

The United States Department of Agriculture (USDA) not only requires excessively high levels of protein in federally subsidized meals, such as those served at day-care centers and school lunch programs, but also buys up "surplus" meat and dairy products that cannot be sold in the open market. The long-term result of these policies is to help establish lifelong eating habits that will later result in an increased incidence of heart disease, cancer, and other degenerative diseases.[41] And, as Dr. Michael Fox points out, there is also an *immediate* risk in feeding children diets high in meat and dairy foods, as there is increasing evidence that these foods play a role in a variety of childhood health problems, including infantile diabetes, attention deficit disorder, and possibly even infantile autism.[42]

The political clout of the livestock growers' lobby is so strong that the USDA has long restricted the amount of soy that can be used in federally subsidized meals in order to maximize the use of beef, pork, and poultry. But in March 2000, the USDA approved the use of soy as a meat substitute in federally subsidized meals for schools and day-care centers.[43]

THE THREAT TO THE ENVIRONMENT

American agriculture produces an amount of animal waste that is 130 to 140 times greater than that which humans produce—five tons of manure for every man, woman, and child in the country. In 1997, it is estimated that farm animals in the United States were generating some 1.37 billion tons of waste *per year*, an amount sufficient to fill enough railroad boxcars to circle the earth twelve and a half times![44, 45, 46]

On factory farms, huge amounts of this manure are heavily concentrated on land that cannot absorb it. The waste is therefore stored in massive earthen lagoons that are up to eight acres in size. These lagoons regularly leak, contaminating rivers, lakes, streams, and groundwater.[47]

One result of producing so much manure without a safe way to dispose of it has been the emergence of a remarkably toxic microbe, *Pfiesteria piscicada*. This microbe has sickened people and caused massive fish kills along the East Coast of the United States, and has also been linked to water pollution because it is activated by excess nutrients from manure and farm runoffs.[48]

In people, *Pfiesteria* can cause a variety of symptoms, including severe headaches, loss of memory and vision, burning sores, and kidney and liver damage, all of which can occur for up to six years after exposure.[49, 50] In 1997, the microbe was found in several tributaries of the Chesapeake Bay, which had to be closed to public access after 30,000 fish were killed. The source was thought to be nutrient runoff from upstream factory poultry farms, which annually produce over 600 million chickens and an immense amount of waste.[51]

That same year in North Carolina, *Pfiesteria* killed 450,000 fish. Most of the fish died after a spill dumped into the New River some 22 million gallons of hog waste—a volume twice the size of the *Exxon Valdez* oil spill. Farm runoff and waste have been found to be polluting half of the nation's watersheds studied by the Environmental Protection Agency (EPA). A 7,728-square mile "dead zone"—an area the size of the State of New Jersey—has formed in the Gulf of Mexico, caused in large part by farm pollution flowing down the Mississippi River. The zone, which is too polluted to support marine life, was found to be 700 square miles larger in July 1999 than it was when measured in 1995.[52, 53]

North Carolina has, in fact, suffered greatly from the industrialization of American agriculture. After the opening of the Smithfield Foods plant in 1991, industrial hog raising in the state mushroomed, growing from 2.5 million hogs to over 10 million. At the same time, the number of hog farms plummeted from 13,000 to less than 5,000, with most of the smaller operators going out of business.[54]

In September of 1999, Hurricanes Dennis and Floyd swept through the eastern part of the state, killing over 2 million chickens, 30,000 hogs, and thousands of other farm animals, and causing waste pits and sewer plants to overflow. Some 1.5 million gallons of manure and urine spilled into a swamp adjoining a tributary of the Cape Fear River. Hog waste from containment ponds was a major contaminant of the floodwaters, along with decomposing chickens, cows, and hogs; farm and lawn fertilizers; raw sewage; decomposing vegetation; and topsoil. [55, 56, 57, 58]

As sludge flowed from the Neuse and Tar Rivers into Pamlico Sound, and from the Cape Fear River into the ocean, huge dead zones were created in the ocean. The largest was a 350-mile expanse of Pamlico Sound and nearby Core Sound. Off Cape Fear, 300 square miles of ocean were contaminated to a depth of 40 feet, causing fear for the long-term health of these areas and their prospects for recovery. As *The New York Times* reported in November 1999, "Now scientists fear the flood has also created an ecological time bomb that could bring disaster":

> They fear for the biologically rich waters that separate the famous Outer Banks from the Carolina mainland. This complex of sounds, bays, and inlets comprises the second largest estuary in the country, after the Chesapeake Bay, and is one of the nation's most important incubators of marine life. . . . [G]reat expanses of the estuary could rapidly be drained of oxygen, killing multitudes of fish and other creatures, and drastically limiting habitat for surviving aquatic life. . . . [I]t could take several years for the situation to play out.[59]

In the meantime, while a few large corporations make a fortune, others suffer the economic consequences. The stench from factory farms has forced some businesses, like day care centers, to close; residential property values have been hurt, with some people unable to sell their homes; and sport and commercial fishing industries are watching fish populations diminish as worries about contamination increase.[60]

FIGHTING FACTORY FARMING

For most of this country's history, family farmers have been the backbone of the nation. Thomas Jefferson called "small landholders" the "most precious part of a state," and believed that governments should try to help them survive. Two centuries later, in December 1999, Vice President Al Gore said while campaigning in Iowa, "I think American agricultural policy should be explicitly aimed at saving the viability of family farming."[61, 62]

Many Americans agree. Across the United States, people and communities are banding together to keep out factory farms. In Kansas, eighteen out of twenty counties voted to exclude new corporate hog farms, and Holt County, Nebraska, approved a moratorium on new chicken and turkey feedlots. Even North Carolina, home of some of the largest factory hog farms, voted a moratorium on certain types of such facilities. [63, 64]

A 1999 nationwide poll of registered voters, sponsored by The HSUS and ten other groups, found deep-seated opposition to the way factory farms operate. Of those questioned, 77 percent expressed strong concerns about the mistreatment of animals on factory farms; 66 percent said they were more likely to support a candidate who would crack down on pollution from such farms; and 68 percent said they would be more likely to vote for a candidate who supported small family farms. An August 1999 poll of Iowa voters conducted for the League of Conservation Voters Education Fund found 87 percent thought it was important to have a presidential candidate who makes environmental protection a top priority; 86 percent worried that waste from factory farms was polluting their water; and 80 percent were more likely to support a candidate who called for tough measures to protect water quality from industrial livestock waste and pesticide runoff.[65, 66]

But despite Gore's statement and the public's opposition to factory farming, it is the factory farmers—not the struggling family farmers—who receive the vast majority of government payments. These payments come in the form of emergency and disaster relief, crop insurance, compensation for low commodity prices—most recently, for hogs—and promotion of commodities for export, which almost exclusively benefit the largest operators. Moreover, the public pays to clean up or absorbs the damages from the massive pollution and depletion of topsoil and other natural resources caused by industrial farming. According to one estimate, in just one decade, from 1986 to 1995, federal support and subsidies for farmers cost taxpayers and consumers $370 billion—enough to buy every farm in forty-one states.[67]

EXPORTING OUR PROBLEMS

International trade is one area where large agribusiness corporations are dominating American agriculture. Gary Valen attributes much of the drive towards "machines, technologies, and the use of animals as commodities" to the "incredible profits" being made by "a few powerful conglomerates" that are exporting agricultural technologies, services, and products—but mainly, farm animals.[68] With a record $60 billion in farm exports in 1996, agriculture ranked number one as the leading positive contributor to the United States trade balance. But, ironically, the world's poorest countries have, themselves, also become big food exporters, exacerbating their poverty levels by concentrating on growing food for export to the rich, industrialized nations. Global agribusiness companies are taking over the fertile lands once used by small farmers to grow staple food crops for themselves and their communities, and are converting the land to grow luxury crops—flowers and exotic fruits, for instance—for export. This leaves formerly self-sufficient farmers without land, jobs, money, or food for themselves or their villages. Instead of feeding the poor and hungry, these farmers are joining their ranks.[69, 70, 71]

Unfortunately, harmful factory farming methods are spreading to developing countries to meet the growing demands for "food security." But there is another way to achieve this goal, says Linda Elswick, co-coordinator of International Partners for Sustainable Agriculture (IPSA), a group at the forefront of the global effort to stop the spread of factory farming abroad. IPSA's mission is to achieve food security through sustainable food and farming systems, and to speak for small-scale family farmers and community-based food security groups. As Elswick says:

> Our experience with factory farming in the U.S. has overwhelmingly demonstrated the advantages of and need for a humane, sustainable agriculture. This is one of the most significant trends in agriculture production today. . . . We have a particular obligation to give voice to successful

alternatives before this model is passed on to those in other countries who are unaware of the costs to animals, to farmers, to the environment and to communities.[72]

It's hard fighting the beef industry with its huge lobbying budget and government subsidies totaling many millions of dollars. For example, in December 1999, the World Bank approved a $93.5 million loan to finance the building in China of 130 feedlots and 5 large processing centers for beef cattle. As pointed out by Dr. Neal D. Barnard, president of the Physicians Committee for Responsible Medicine, the promotion of cattle farming in China will do more than result in a massive waste of grain. It will also promote poor health by changing "the traditional Chinese diet . . . that has kept heart disease and myriad other western health problems at arm's length."[73]

PLAYING GENETIC ROULETTE

Another threat to traditional farming is genetic engineering. The transformation of animals and plants into hybrid creatures in order to increase profits and production seems like something out of science fiction. Unfortunately, it's real, it's here, and its dangers may not be known until it is too late to do anything about them.

Are We Building a Better Food Supply?

A powerful movement is underway to genetically restructure our food supply, and hundreds of bioengineered foods are being developed and are appearing on our grocery shelves, untested and unlabeled as to their origins. Already, half of all soybeans, a third to a fourth of the corn crop, and many of the potatoes grown by United States farmers have been genetically altered. And there are plans to produce many more modified vegetables, including broccoli, alfalfa, cabbage, and lettuce.[74]

Genes are the basic physical units of heredity, and carry the genetic codes that form future generations. When genes are altered and tampered with, they can create mutated life forms that never before existed. These altered life forms can then multiply and spread across the globe, causing damage that can never be repaired.

Often, scientists try to "improve" plants or animals by inserting into them a gene from another creature to speed up or increase growth, for example. The results have been the creations of toma-toes with flounder genes, fish and pigs with human genes, and fish engineered with genes from cattle, chickens, and even humans. But what happens when such hybrids escape or are released into the wild, and mate with or crowd out native species? No one knows the answer, and by the time anyone does, it may be too late to save the gene pool.[75, 76, 77]

Bioengineered animals often experience great suffering and are unable to function as nature intended. One "super salmon" had a massive head and was unable to swim, eat, or breathe naturally. A "super pig" could neither walk nor stand. In 1999, scientists suc-ceeded in injecting jellyfish genes into mice and monkey embryos, techniques which experimenters said could be used to create mon-keys with human genes or even to add nonhuman genes to human embryos. Many other animals have been subjected to similarly grotesque alterations in the name of genetic engineering, and some have even been patented by the firms that produced them.[78, 79] Similarly, cloning—such as that used to create the lamb named Dolly in 1997—has been used to engineer new creatures to serve human needs: mice with human ears; frogs without heads; cows, goats, and sheep that produce milk that is more "humanized."[80]

In the new and largely unstudied, untested field of agricultur-al biotechnology, we have not only opened Pandora's box, but we are emptying it into the environment. Literally hundreds of thou-sands of genetically engineered living organisms whose behavior is unpredictable have already been produced and released on over 90 million acres. Millions more will be released over the next few years.[81]

Food crops have been developed that have the "benefit" of being able to resist and survive herbicides. But it is yet to be determined what would happen if one of these plants cross-pollinated with a harmful weed, conferring its herbicide resistance on the pest plant, which could then turn into a "super-weed." Similarly, pesticide resistance could be transferred to insects, creating "super-bugs."[82]

The use of herbicide-resistant crops has led to a much heavier and more frequent use of toxic herbicides. Organic farmer Freder-ick Kirschenmann points out that it is becoming increasingly diffi-cult to raise a garden in rural areas—even on his North Dakota farm—because of the drift from nearby spraying, which now takes place all year-round due to genetically engineered crops.[83] In this way, such technology is increasing the toxicity of our environment, subjecting our crops, and ourselves, to regular exposure to deadly chemicals.

Biotechnology corporations have even succeeded in threatening the future effectiveness of natural, nontoxic pesticides such as *Bacillus thuringiensis* (Bt). Bt, which is harmless to humans and breaks down rapidly in sunlight, is widely used by organic farmers. Scientists have inserted Bt genes into plants to make them resistant to insects. However, when insects are exposed to Bt or other pesticides over long periods—as they would be via these genetically altered plants—they tend to develop immunity to the pesticides, making the substances useless against harmful insects.

Gene-altered plants like those just described may also be dangerous to beneficial, desirable insects. For instance, corn that has been genetically altered with Bt to kill corn-boring caterpillars, may also be killing monarchs and other butterflies. The hybrid corn, introduced in 1996, now constitutes a third to a fourth of the nation's corn crop. It is planted on 10 to 20 million acres in the path of the monarchs' annual migration. Half of the monarchs that migrate to Mexico for the winter are born in the United States corn belt, and live on milkweed found around the fields of pollinating corn.[84, 85, 86] Pollen from the corn blows onto nearby milkweed plants, which monarch larvae feed upon exclusively. In tests performed by Cornell University scientists, monarch larvae were fed milkweed sprinkled with Bt pollen. Within four days, 44 percent were dead, and the rest were small and lethargic. Other monarch larvae eating regular pollen showed no such ill effects. No one can tell what the long-term effects of Bt corn will be on the already struggling population of monarchs—or, for that matter, on the humans who eat the corn.[87, 88, 89]

Are We Harming Our Own Health?

While defenders of genetic engineering claim that bioengineered foods pose no *known* health risks to consumers, everyone agrees that there have not been any long-term studies of these products. The Food and Drug Administration (FDA) does not test such products, accepting assurances from manufacturers that their products are safe. Even Secretary of Agriculture Dan Glickman, a strong promoter of genetic engineering, has acknowledged that the federal agencies responsible for the safety of such food—the USDA,

FDA, and EPA—do not have sufficient staff or resources to undertake testing of these products.[90, 91]

Europeans have strongly resisted pressure from the United States to buy American farm products like corn and soybeans, much of which are genetically altered. Since natural corn cannot be readily distinguished from the altered varieties, United States exports to Europe virtually ceased in the late 1990s, costing American farmers some $200 million annually. As a result, some major food exporters, such as Archer Daniels Midland, announced that they would stop buying bioengineered corn. The company then told farmers to go back to growing natural corn.[92, 93]

The United States government's response to European fears of American products was to pressure Europe to accept such foods, taking its case to the World Trade Organization (WTO). There, it won a ruling which stated that Europe could not ban any American beef treated with hormones that are suspected of causing cancer.[94, 95]

In Europe, approval of genetically modified crops essentially halted in mid-1998. Studies by European scientists had demonstrated that the consumption of dairy products from cows treated with bovine growth hormone (rBGH) may increase the risk of cancers of the breast, colon, and prostate.[96, 97]

Genetically engineered foods may also cause allergies in susceptible individuals, especially when people with food allergies unknowingly eat "safe" food that has been genetically engineered with genes from an allergy-producing food. A study in *The New England Journal of Medicine* demonstrated how people who were allergic to nuts experienced serious reactions when eating soybeans that, unknown to them, contained a gene from a Brazil nut.[98] And in October 1999, the prestigious medical journal *The Lancet* released a study reporting that animals fed genetically altered potatoes experienced changes in their intestines. The study was part of a larger research project conducted by Dr. Arpad Pusztai, a controversial British scientist who stated that animals fed bioengineered potatoes experienced immune system problems and stunted organ growth.[99]

Don't We Have the Right to Know?

Unfortunately, the FDA has refused to require that genetically altered food be so labeled, making it virtually impossible for those who want to avoid such products to do so. Millions of Americans, including infants and children, are unknowingly consuming such foods, despite overwhelming public opposition to genetic engineering and the secrecy surrounding it.

A February 1997 Time/CNN poll found that three out of four Americans think that research into human cloning is "against the will of God." In a 1999 survey of consumers sponsored by the Swiss food and drug firm Novartis, over 90 percent said they favored labeling of genetically modified products. A petition to the FDA asking for mandatory labeling of such foods was signed by over 500,000 people. And when the Department of Agriculture proposed regulations on what foods could be labeled "organic," over 280,000 people opposed including foods that had been genetically altered.[100, 101]

Largely as a result of public opinion and pressure from environmental and animal protection groups, some progress is being made in slowing down the race towards massive bioengineering. The Gerber Baby Food Company has dropped genetically modified corn and soybeans from its line of products. In October 1999, Monsanto announced that it would abandon plans to commercialize its "terminator" gene, which creates plants whose seeds are sterile. This technology would produce huge profits for seed companies by preventing farmers from saving seeds for future plantings. But, amazingly, the USDA continues to promote "terminator technology," and is still funding research on it.[102, 103, 104]

Despite a few setbacks for the industry, genetically engineered plants and animals continue to be created by the millions. Biotech foods are proliferating, as are the threats to human health and the environment. These problems with biotechnology stem largely from our callous lack of concern for animals. As Dr. Michael Fox puts it, treating animals as "disposable commodities of human creation . . . further erodes the ethic of respect for the intrinsic value and sanctity of individual life, a principle that is critical to the future well-being of both humans and other animals."[105, 106]

THE RAVAGES OF AGRICULTURE

Agriculture is such a massive and dominant enterprise that it must be taken very seriously by society, pursued very carefully by farmers, and followed very closely by policymakers. Farming and ranching occupy at least a third of the world's land mass and a majority of the "useable" land, when one excludes deserts and mountain ranges. In the United States, perhaps 45 percent or more of the land is devoted to raising animals and the crops needed to feed them.[107] And the effects of this widespread activity has been both drastic and frightening.

An Industry of Destruction

The pervasive presence across the globe of farming—especially livestock raising—carries with it a huge potential for damage and destruction. In many areas, farming is drastically distorting the use and distribution of food and natural resources. Instead of helping to feed the world's hungry people, it is contributing to their malnutrition and starvation, while ruining the land for future generations. An August 1991 study by the United Nations Environment Program revealed that 73 percent of the world's rangelands had been seriously damaged from overgrazing by livestock, and that up to 80 percent of western rangelands in the United States—700 million acres—were being turned into desert, mainly from overgrazing.[108]

There is nothing new about such destructive agricultural practices. In 1953, the Department of Agriculture's Soil Conservation Service published "Conquest of the Land Through 7,000 Years." A 1938 to 1939 report issued by its former assistant chief, W.C. Lowdermilk, described how, over the millennia, bad agricultural practices have "helped topple empires and wipe out entire civilizations."[109]

Some of the worst problems have been caused by livestock and their overgrazing. For centuries, overgrazing has caused soil erosion, deforestation, and general abuse of the land. Lowdermilk concluded that "if civilization is to avoid a long decline, like the one that has blighted North Africa and the Near East for thirteen centuries, society must be born again out of an economy of exploitation, into an economy of conservation."[110]

An Industry of Waste

Many of our present unsustainable agricultural practices would shock even Lowdermilk. The case can be made that raising animals for food is now the leading cause of environmental degradation and resource depletion throughout the world. It is livestock raising, more than all other human activities combined, that helps deplete topsoil, groundwater, and energy resources, while ravaging forests, waterways, wildlife, and habitat.

More than half of the water we use in this country goes towards livestock production, including the irrigation of feed crops and pasture grass, consumption by livestock, and waste disposal. Animal agriculture uses more water than all American cities and industries combined. It takes 2,500 to 6,000 gallons of water to produce one pound of meat, but only 25 gallons of water to grow one pound of wheat.[111]

Livestock raising also consumes large amounts of grain. About 70 percent of the wheat and other grains grown in this country—some 300 million tons—is fed not to Americans or the world's starving masses, but to livestock and poultry. Very little of this food grain comes back to us in the form of meat. A chicken has to eat five pounds of protein to produce one pound of protein from chicken flesh—an 80-percent waste of food. The production of a pound of pork protein requires the consumption of seven and a half pounds of protein. And to produce one pound of feedlot beef, a cow has to eat sixteen pounds of grain and soybeans—a 94-percent waste![112, 113]

Doesn't it make more sense for *humans* to eat that grain—which is healthier and more nutritious than meat—and to feed it to the world's 800 million hungry people, than to waste so much of it on livestock?

Squandering Our Heritage

Given the wasteful, inhumane, and unsustainable way in which our agricultural system is evolving, we are clearly on the verge of squandering, and perhaps losing forever, the bountiful system that helped make this country great. In doing so, we are destroying the combination of factors that have allowed our country to attain an unprecedented level of prosperity: free markets, vital rural communities, soil productivity, and the essential link between farmers, animals, and the land that once gave such integrity to this enterprise.

As the 1997 Soul of Agriculture conference noted in its "Call to Action" statement, "Many widespread agricultural practices, particularly those that seek to maximize production without any thought to other values, are destroying the capacity of good farmland to continue to produce for generations to come":

Thoughtless sprawl that paves over productive land, practices that allow significant erosion, and industrially intensive agriculture that destroys the biotic community of living soil, are just a few of the practices that will take food from the mouths of our children and grandchildren. [114]

Once farmland and topsoil are lost, they cannot be recovered. Currently, the rural landscape is disappearing at a rate of 3 million acres a year, according to the United States Department of Agriculture. Between 1992 and 1997, some 16 million acres were lost to development—which is double the previous rate.[115, 116]

Since 1995, cropland has been losing soil to erosion at a rate of 1.9 billion tons a year. Worldwide, the annual loss of topsoil is estimated at over 25 billion tons. We cannot continue down this dead-end road without arriving at a destination that will strand our children in a hollow and ravaged landscape.[117, 118]

In some ways, our soil is the basis of civilization itself. In *Out of the Earth—Civilization and the Life of the Soil*, Daniel Hillel writes, "The depth of the entire soil profile, though it varies, is generally not much more than one meter [39.37 inches] deep. So incredibly thin, and vulnerable, is this outer layer of the earth's crust that supports all terrestrial life."[119]

To produce just one inch of fertile topsoil can take five centuries. But in the last four decades of employing industrial production techniques that emphasize the use of chemicals and machines, the United States has lost 50 percent of its topsoil. Any short-term production gains squeezed from the soil have come at the expense of long-term depletion of the land and future starvation of people—especially that half of the world's population comprised of people who depend on the crops they grow for themselves and their communities.[120]

We are profoundly ignorant about the nature of the living, complex, biotic community that we call soil. As Paul and Anne Ehrlich point out in their book *Extinction*, "The diversity of organisms in a small bit of soil is truly astonishing":

In about a square yard of a Danish pasture soil, some 45,000 small earthworm relatives, 10 million roundworms, and 48,000 tiny insects and mites were found. A gram of fertile agricultural soil has yielded over 30,000 one-celled animals, 50,000 algae, 400,000 fungi, and over 2.5 billion bacteria. The importance of these tiny living components of the soil cannot be overestimated.[121]

Jan Hartke observes, "We need to instill in the public, and especially our young people who will be the future stewards of the soil, a new and realistic perspective about the life force of the soil. Any society that does not respect and revere its soil will doom itself, and much of the biodiversity of the planet."[122]

A VISION OF SUSTAINABLE AGRICULTURE

The need for a new agricultural policy—a new vision of farming—is clear. Many farmers, ethicists, and environmentalists agree that this is the only way we can save our planet and ourselves.

Returning to Traditional Values

One of the pioneers in promoting a new ethic for sustainable agriculture is Frederick Kirschenmann, who for a quarter of a century has pursued such practices on his family's biodynamic, 3,100-acre wheat and cattle farm in North Dakota. In a 1993 article in the quarterly publication *Earth Ethics*, he described what is at stake in this evolving debate over agriculture:

> If the act of farming is to continue without destroying the web of life and its resource base, it must be done in a manner that respects all of life and the environment. In other words, farming must be done in a manner that restores what is used up in the process of production. In essence, that is what is meant by sustainable agriculture.[123]

Kirschenmann explained that "our current food system is principally controlled by multinational food companies," which "seek a business climate that offers cheap labor, cheap raw materials, and the least environmental restrictions." But these business principles, he notes, are diametrically opposed to "farming *with* nature," in which "the farmer must seek to restore the resource base, protect the environment, and maintain qualified husbandry on the land."[124]

Richard Clugston sees America's rural crisis as "a symptom of the moral and spiritual crisis of America," with "decision-making being driven by finding the lowest price, the greatest short-term financial return, and the greatest increase in productivity." But, he warns, "only by creating policies, plans, and consumer choices that consciously value ecological soundness, social justice, and humaneness—even if it sacrifices some short-term economic gain—can we create truly vital rural communities." Otherwise, he says, "rural America will most likely become a depleted, denuded, 'third world'—not the revitalized heartland, producing wholesome food that the Founding Fathers regarded as the moral fiber of the United States."[125]

What is needed, of course, is neither new nor radical, but rather a return to the traditional practices of conscientious family farmers, who cared for their animals and their land. Today, we call this *humane sustainable agriculture* (HSA), which The HSUS's "Humane Consumer and Producer Guide" says "produces adequate amounts of safe, wholesome food in a manner that is ecologically sound, economically viable, equitable, and humane." The guide continues, "HSA meets farm animals' basic physical and behavioral requirements for health and well-being through a food and agricultural system that respects all of nature—humans, soil, water, plants, and animals, wild as well as domestic."[126]

In 1990, the Global Tomorrow Coalition in Washington, D.C., published an agenda for helping farmers and communities move towards a sustainable future. It includes the following recommendations:

❑ Promote and fund agro-ecology, which includes crop rotation, nontoxic pest management, windbreaks, water conservation, renewable energy sources, and on-site nutrient recycling.

❑ Teach school children sustainable principles for nature, gardening, and farming.

❑ Use tax incentives to encourage local food production and support small farms.

❑ Incorporate the concept of self-reliance into community planning by emphasizing the inclusion of gardens, trees, alternative energy and transportation, and local job opportunities.[127]

A New Agricultural Ethic

In March 1997, a committee of twenty farmers, ethicists, academics, environmentalists, and religious leaders came together in the Soul of Agriculture project. Established by the Center for Respect of Life and Environment and The HSUS, this project sought to develop and promote a new agricultural production ethic for the twenty-first century. From this meeting came agreement on a set of shared values that can serve as the foundation for a new farming ethic. This ethic would be based on the idea that a good farmer "works hard and wastes nothing; loves the land as well as posterity; is a citizen of the community and a steward of nature; and engages in work that keeps faith with all creation."[128]

The project's participants agreed on a number of values:

1. A new ethic in agriculture begins with an understanding of the sanctity of Creation. We must stop treating farm animals, the land, and farmers themselves as machines, rather than as living, valuable entities. . . . We have been blessed with a bountiful and beautiful land, and with that gift comes a responsibility to care for it as best we can, understanding all the while that our comprehension of this infinitely complex system is extremely limited. . . .

2. Stewardship-based production of food, clothing, and shelter is a good and essential use of the land in our trust. . . . It is important to value farming as an honorable endeavor that has a place in the landscape. . . . Farming must be seen as an integral part of appropriate rural landscapes and communities, and have a place in it for wildness.

3. Food is different from other things that we produce. Agriculture is arguably the only human practice that touches everyone, every day. Agriculture serves to unite all of humanity with each other and with the planet. . . . A new production ethic will celebrate food and environmental protection as inseparable goals.

4. Farming has a responsibility to the future. . . . Farming should move to an ideal of being ever-renewing, replacing what it takes from the land and leaving no waste. . . . [I]t is immoral for us to meet our current needs in ways that diminish the capacity of future generations to meet theirs. . . . [P]ractices that build the soil, enhance biological diversity, and increase our knowledge of how to

farm in partnership with nature all construct a legacy that can serve future generations and the land long after we are gone.[129]

The project reached still other conclusions about farming ethics and values:

❏ Stability comes from communities that understand and value what farms and farmers do, and participate in the culture of agriculture;

❏ Diversity is a strength; raising a variety of crops makes a farm more self-supporting, and less dependent upon outside help to keep insects, weeds, and other pests in check;

❏ Farmland should be owned and managed by the people who live on it, and they should be able to earn a decent livelihood from that land. . . . Ownership gives farmers a strong incentive to protect the long-term health and productivity of the land.

❏ The beauty of rural landscapes is a national treasure, and we must adopt a new understanding of the intrinsic, independent value of beauty to the proper function of civilization.[130]

In short, the new agricultural production ethic holds that "good agriculture contributes to the stability, beauty, and integrity of the human and natural community of life with which it interacts. It is not only economically viable, and socially just, it also stewards the land, and respects the needs of future generations."[131]

Restoring Soil and Soul

There is much at stake here in adopting a new agricultural ethic. Tom Frantzen, who runs a 335-acre farm outside Alta Vista, Iowa, naturally and humanely raises hogs and cattle and a variety of crops and animal feed. Frantzen calls sustainable agriculture "the issue of our lifetime. . . . The development of a food system that is ecologically humane and sociologically sound is the greatest cause there is."[132]

Kentucky farmer Wendell Berry, who has been involved with farming and rural decline issues for thirty-six years, writes, "A policy that destroys farmers and farmland cannot be acceptable in agricultural terms":

> This also directly contradicts our goal of national defense. A country that heedlessly is destroying its capacity to feed itself cannot be defended . . . I cannot see why a healthful, dependable, ecologically sound farm-and-farmer conserving agricultural economy is not a primary goal of this country.[133]

Thomas Berry stresses how essential good farming is to humans, and the "absolute interdependence" of all living beings, in which the sequence of "dissolution and renewal . . . has continued for billions of years," via the "capacity for self-renewal through seeds that bond each generation of plants to the next":

> Every animal form depends ultimately on plant forms that alone can transform the energy of the sun and the minerals of earth into the living substance needed for the life nourishment of the entire animal world, including the human community. The well-being of the soil must be the primary concern for humans.[134]

"To disrupt this process," Berry warns, "is to break the Covenant of the Earth and to imperil life itself."[135]

These issues are of such importance that it is essential to make people understand how critical they are to the survival of our society. Richard Clugston notes that the rural crisis can be addressed only through a major effort to achieve rural revitalization through sustainable, self-reliant strategies of the kind discussed above. He further states that "this will require a value shift from the deeply American notion that land is just a commodity, to recognizing that land is primarily a community of living beings and a common trust."[136]

Robert F. Welborn, who practices law in Denver and runs an organic farm nearby, contends that "if we want quality of life for the future, quality agriculture is our most practical and most ethical means." And he believes that the best way of achieving this objective is to "accept that human beings are not the only important living things on earth, and [to] accept the inter-relatedness of all life. Our goal is to protect the integrity of that inter-relatedness and preserve and enhance the life and beauty of our planet."[137]

For 10,000 years at least, farming has been central to human society. In our uniquely human way, we have tenaciously pursued this activity in a manner that has shaped and dominated the planet. We cannot now drastically change the nature of farming without also fundamentally changing the nature of our society.

We should at least be aware of what we are doing and where we are going before we irrevocably commit to such a profound reordering of our values, our economy, and our environment, for this is the legacy we will hand down to our children. Let us hope that we have the foresight to understand that society as we know it is at serious risk, and to act before time runs out on us all.

PART III

Our Inhumane Society

4. HUNTING—
SPORT OR SLAUGHTER?

Every year across America, hunters legally kill over 100 million creatures, mainly for the fun of it. They call it "sport."[1, 2] Not counted in this disturbing fact are the millions of animals that are illegally killed and never reported. Neither does it include those animals who are injured and, although able to get away, are destined to suffer a slow and agonizing death.

Sport hunting is vigorously promoted, supported, and subsidized by state and federal governments as a healthy, character-building outdoor activity. It is touted as a valuable learning activity for young people. But as we shall see, hunting actually has a severely detrimental impact on our society that goes way beyond the violent treatment of the helpless animals that are its primary victims.

THE MAGNITUDE OF THE SLAUGHTER

Of all the issues facing the conservation community, none is more controversial and contentious than sport hunting. To truly understand why feelings are so strong on this issue, one must be aware of the number of blameless, defenseless animals that are shot, wounded, maimed, crippled, and orphaned each year by hunters. We do shameful things to wild animals that we would never think of doing to our pets or even to our domestic livestock. Yet we perform these atrocities every year on tens of millions of creatures who deserve just as much respect as our pet dogs, cats, and birds.

It is estimated that, conservatively, over a 100 million wild birds and mammals are legally killed and reported each year. This toll includes (give or take a few million): 25 million doves, 16 million squirrels, 13 million quail, 11 million rabbits, 10 million pheasants, 10 million ducks, 9 million deer, 2 million woodchucks, 2 million geese, 600,000 crows, 500,000 prairie dogs, 300,000 coots, 61,000 skunks, 20,000 black bears, 800 swans, and 500 wolverines.[3, 4]

These figures are in fact much lower than the actual toll, since they represent only those deaths reported by the states based on hunter surveys. They do not include animals that are poached, eventually die from wounds, or are killed by out-of-state hunters.[5]

WIPING OUT WILDLIFE

Hunting is almost religiously defended by its proponents, including many conservationists, as beneficial and even essential to the welfare of wildlife. Its supporters claim that hunting is necessary to help raise money for conservation and habitat protection. They also maintain it prevents the overpopulation of game animals, especially deer. However, as it is currently practiced in the United States and abroad, hunting not only fails to conserve the animals involved, it also represents a serious threat to the survival of many wildlife species.

For millennia, hunting has helped wipe out entire animal populations. For instance, it is believed that early North American aboriginal hunters were largely responsible for wiping out many of the continent's large Pleistocene mammals, such as the mammoth; mastodon; long-necked camel; giant lion, bear, and wolf; as well as the 400-pound beaver and seven-foot-tall bison.[6, 7]

Naturally, hunting became increasingly damaging with the modernization of weapons. By the second half of the nineteenth century, the wide availability of repeating rifles put almost every wild creature somewhere within the range of sport and commercial hunters. This resulted in the widespread destruction of much of the country's wildlife.

Passenger pigeons were once the most populous bird species

in North America. Flocks flying overhead would blacken the sky for days at a time. In the 1860s and 1870s, tens of millions of these birds were shot each year. This massive killing, combined with widespread destruction of their nesting areas, brought about the extinction of this species in the early 1900s.[8, 9]

Many buffalo, or American bison, were shot and killed for sport, often by men riding on horseback or on trains. Subsequently, the animals were left to rot, depriving the Plains Indians of their means of survival. Market hunters also killed buffalo for their hides, their meat, and even for their tongues. The population of this animal was reduced from an estimated 60 to 90 million, to just a few hundred by the late 1800s.[10, 11]

In the southern United States, the demand for plumage by the millinery trade led to the massive sport and commercial slaughter of egrets, great white herons, roseate spoonbills, and other beautiful birds. This drastically and permanently reduced their numbers, in some cases to the point of near extinction.[12]

Hunting is also directly responsible for helping to eliminate many other animals, including the heath hen, eastern elk, Merriam elk, Carolina parakeet, Eskimo curlew, and Badlands bighorn.

WILDLIFE MANAGEMENT

By the 1930s, public concern over the massive destruction of wildlife forced the adoption of laws and regulations to control and "manage" the killing of wild animals. Hunters played an important role in this change, which essentially substituted regulated sport hunting for the formerly unrestrained commercial or market hunting of animals. A new science, wildlife management, was established. It was largely credited to Aldo Leopold (1887–1948)—a hunter and naturalist of almost legendary stature within the conservation community.

According to the tenets of modern wildlife management, wildlife is considered a natural resource to be managed much like agricultural crops, the surplus of which should be regularly "harvested." Limits on the kill would be based on the carrying capacity of the habitat and the ability of the species to reproduce itself. This would help to avoid depleting the animals or allowing them to overpopulate. The various states, through their fish and game departments and commissions, would have the primary role in managing wildlife. The federal government would later assume responsibility for certain other species, such as migratory waterfowl.

The adoption and wide acceptance of this wildlife-management structure throughout the nation was instrumental in controlling the killing of many species of wildlife and saving them from disappearing. However, the killing of wolves and other predatory species continued unabated.

Ever since, hunters and their minions have essentially run state wildlife agencies and, to a large extent, the United States Fish and Wildlife Service (FWS) as well. The result has been the almost mindless promotion of recreational hunting over other "non-consumptive" activities, such as bird watching and other types of wildlife observation, and to the exclusion of such recreational activities as hiking and camping.

HUNTING ENDANGERED WILDLIFE

The hunting establishment and the wildlife management lobby insist that they are the true conservationists and are responsible for saving rare species, not threatening them. In fact, legal, officially sanctioned, government-supported hunting is still helping to imperil the survival of many vanishing species.

In the United States, open hunting seasons were held for grizzly bears in Montana and black bears in Florida through the early 1990s, until they were stopped through lawsuits by animal protection groups. Florida still permits hunting of the rare Sherman's fox squirrel, as well as large-scale hunting in the Big Cypress National Preserve, which is the prime remaining refuge for the most endangered mammal in North America—the Florida panther. Although only twenty-five to fifty of these panthers are still in existence, Florida law still permits hunters in the Preserve to shoot large numbers of wild hogs and deer. This depletes the panthers' main food supply, disrupting their habitat and sometimes causing them to wander into areas where they are vulnerable to danger, such as being hit by cars.

Loose regulations and the multitude of hunters swarming over wetlands almost guarantee that protected species of waterfowl will be shot accidentally. For example, hunting is permitted throughout much of the flyway used by the endangered whooping crane as it migrates from Canada to Texas. Hunters begin shooting before dawn and continue through sunset, and it is extremely difficult for even the most experienced hunters to differentiate waterfowl species. Therefore, the occasional, unintentional shootings of whoopers are not surprising. And since it is illegal to shoot them, many killings go unreported. With only a few hundred whoopers in captivity and the wild, we can ill afford to lose even a few to confused sportsmen.

Illegal shooting has also helped reduce the population of our threatened national symbol, the bald eagle. Studies over the years have documented this factor as one of the major causes for eagle losses. Other species that have been endangered in large part by hunting include the tiger, jaguar, sable antelope, spectacled bear, and grizzly bear. Numerous foreign endangered species also continue to be hunted by American "sportsmen."[13]

WHO PAYS FOR CONSERVATION?

One of the most frequently cited defenses of hunting is that it makes an important contribution in buying and preserving critical habitat for wildlife. This is done primarily as the result of two landmark laws enacted in the 1930s—The Duck Stamp Act and The Pittman-Robertson Act.

The Duck Stamp Act uses revenue from waterfowl hunting permits to acquire wetlands, which are essential for the breeding of waterfowl and many other creatures. Some hunting groups, mainly Ducks Unlimited, are also active in purchasing and protecting waterfowl habitat.

The Pittman-Robertson Act provides money to state fish and wildlife agencies for "game management" and "wildlife restoration" by taxing sales of arms and ammunition. State wildlife agencies get their funding from the sale of hunting and fishing licenses and usually put up one matching dollar for every three federal dollars received. Therefore, although hunters are a small minority of the population, state and federal wildlife officials consider them to be their main constituency. After all, they help pay the salaries of fish and game agency employees, and they are the main source of their funding.

The revenues involved are considerable, and hunters repeatedly claim that this money funds conservation programs throughout the nation, particularly habitat acquisition. In 1999, approximately $165 million was distributed, including $27 million for "hunter education," which includes programs that recruit young hunters.[14]

Despite these claims, closer examination of the funds reveals that, over the years, only a small percentage of the revenue raised has been spent on buying wetlands and other wildlife habitat. Much larger amounts have been used for other, often environmentally destructive activities.

This was made clear when, in 1975, a lawsuit by an animal protection group, Friends of Animals, forced the United States Department of the Interior's Fish and Wildlife Service to draft an Environmental Impact Statement (EIS) on the federal aid for fish and wildlife restoration program. The report revealed that only about one-seventh of the funds were spent on buying habitat for wildlife.[15] Much of the rest of the money—tens of millions of dollars—were used for habitat destruction and degradation in the form of road building and maintenance, pesticide spraying, fencing, timber cutting and burning, bulldozing, and other such activities that harm, rather than help, most wildlife. These expenditures were intended to make the hunting as convenient as possible for the sportsmen, and to generate a maximum number—a "harvestable surplus"—of deer and ducks, often at the expense of other animals.[16]

Obviously, far too much money that is earmarked for "conservation" is instead being used to damage and destroy nature's wildlife habitat. As naturalist Bil Gilbert has written, "The sports hunting establishment is the most pampered, privileged, subsidized recreational group in existence."

THE ECONOMIC VALUE OF WILDLIFE

From an economic standpoint, wildlife has enormous "non-consumptive" value. This is seen in the form of tourism, birdwatching, and other types of harmless recreation that are often incompatible with hunting but involve far greater numbers of people and money spent.

Every few years, the Department of the Interior publishes its "National Survey of Fishing, Hunting, and Wildlife-Associated Recreation," which reveals overwhelming public support for "nonconsumptive wildlife recreation." The latest survey shows that in

1996 "62.9 million people [16 years and older] enjoyed at least one type of wildlife-watching recreational activity, including observing, feeding, or photographing fish and other wildlife in the United States." In contrast, less than a quarter of that number—14 million (about 6 percent)—hunted. Of the $101 billion spent that year on wildlife-associated recreation, wildlife watchers spent $29 billion, which was $8 billion more than the hunters spent.[17] In 1998, over 286 million people visited America's national parks, where hunting is generally banned.

Clearly, if the survival of animals is to be based on their economic value, they are worth much more being shot with a camera instead of a gun. As John A. Hoyt points out in his book *Animals in Peril*, "It is becoming increasingly clear that if wildlife must be used, the best way to 'sustainably utilize' wild animals for profit is through nature-oriented tourism. . . ." He continues:

> Unpersecuted wildlife can, over the long-term, indeed for perpetuity, be an invaluable source of income, employment, and economic development through such non-consumptive activities as photographic safaris and scientific study projects and expeditions. . . . Wiping out creatures that can attract tourists and bring in income for the indefinite future, as is now being done in many areas, is a prime example of killing the proverbial goose that lays the golden egg.[18]

Numerous studies show that wild animals are usually worth much more alive than they are dead. This is especially true in poor nations that need to attract tourist dollars. A 1982 study of Kenya's 150 square mile Amboseli National Park found immense value in the ability of its wildlife to attract tourists. Each lion, it was estimated, was worth $27,000 a year in tourist revenues. The park's elephants brought in $610,000 annually. (Later studies have shown the average value of a single elephant may be up to 1 million dollars.) It was further calculated that the park, when used for wildlife viewing, was worth fifty times more than if it were converted for agricultural use—something parks throughout Africa are constantly being pressured to allow.[19] The potential for wildlife viewing to generate revenues is enormous. Ecotourism is the fastest-growing segment of travel and tourism, generating over $4 trillion dollars a year.

UNSPORTSMANLIKE CONDUCT

There is little "sporting" about modern hunting. Buffalo, for example, are "hunted" by sportsmen who walk up to the unsuspecting animals and shoot them. The famous naturalist Henry David Thoreau (1817–1862) gave an account of moose hunting in his essay "The Maine Woods":

> This hunting of the moose merely for the satisfaction of killing him—not even for the sake of his hide—without making any extraordinary exertion or running any risk yourself, is too much like going out by night to some pasture and shooting your neighbor's horses.
>
> These are God's own horses, poor timid creatures that run fast enough as soon as they smell you. Joe told us of some hunters who a year or two before had shot down several oxen by night, somewhere in the Maine woods, mistaking them for moose, as might any of the hunters; and what is the difference in the sport, but the name?[20]

Aldo Leopold, the father of wildlife management, is a frequently-cited epic figure of the hunting establishment. In his classic work of the 1940s, *A Sand County Almanac*, he wrote of the remorse he felt after shooting a mother wolf who had been playing with her cubs:

> All joined in a welcoming melee of wagging tails and playful maulings. What was literally a pile of wolves writhed and tumbled in the center of an open flat at the foot of our rimrock.
>
> In those days, we had never heard of passing up a chance to kill a wolf. In a second, we were pumping lead into the pack. . . . When our rifles were empty, the old wolf was down, and a pup was dragging a leg into impassable slide-rocks.
>
> We reached the old wolf in time to watch a fierce green fire dying in her eyes. I realized then, and have known ever since, that there was something new to me in those eyes—something known only to her and to the mountain.[21]

THE THRILL OF THE HUNT

For many hunters, having to pursue animals that might get away is too much of a challenge. To cater to these so-called sportsmen, there are over 1,000 "canned" hunting facilities in the United States in which animals (mostly exotic) who have been bought from circuses or zoos, or raised in captivity, are confined in cages or large enclosures and then "stalked" by sportsmen. These "he-men" pay big bucks to experience the thrill of the hunt without having to deal with the agony of missing their quarry.[22]

Many of the animals (some of which are tame and unafraid of humans) who are hunted in these special facilities die a slow and painful death. Although a shot in the animal's head or chest would provide quick death, it also might damage the "trophy," so the hunter typically aims his bullets in other areas of the animal's body.

These guaranteed kills are quite costly for the "adventure-loving" sportsman. A Cape buffalo costs approximately $5,000. For the pleasure of killing a gazelle, the cost is anywhere from $800 to $3,500; a red deer runs from $1,500 to $6,000; and $325 is the price for an angora goat. The most expensive animals of all—lions, tigers, and endangered North African antelopes such as the addax and scimitar-horned oryx—can run in the tens of thousands of dollars.[23]

For other so-called sportsmen who want to avoid even the exertion of pulling the trigger on a captive animal, there is fox-penning. For this, hunters release their dogs to chase and tear to pieces foxes and coyotes who are enclosed within a fenced area. The thrill is said to be in sitting and listening to the baying hounds chasing the terrified prey.[24] This and other forms of hunting have had particularly harmful effects on public health, as they have helped spread rabies across the eastern United States. In the late 1970s, several hunting clubs near the Virginia-West Virginia border brought in rabid raccoons from Florida, causing the mid-Atlantic region's first known epidemic of rabies. Once confined only to the South, this rabies epidemic spread all the way up the eastern United States into New Hampshire. It has created a major health crisis for which there is no known solution.[25]

Ironically, in 1994, a new form of rabies was introduced into the state of Florida. It was caused by hunters who brought a fox pen into Alachua County that contained at least one rabid coyote from southern Texas. Soon, several hounds that were released into the pen became infected and spread the rabies. Eventually, twenty-four people had to undergo the long and painful rabies treatment, and at considerable cost to the public.[26]

WILDLIFE MANAGEMENT'S GREATEST SUCCESSES

Hunters often dismiss their critics as being emotional and unin-formed. But even the classic examples of successful wildlife man-agement—regenerating the populations of deer and waterfowl—are subject to dispute and debate.

Hunters claim that there are more deer in America today than at any other time, and that without hunting pressure, deer would seriously overpopulate and destroy their habitats. But deer num-bers are often kept high by the clear-cutting of forests and other techniques that harm other species. Deer populations have grown in many areas largely because of the elimination of old-growth forests and predators, especially wolves. In Alaska, wolves are still being killed off by the state. This is to stimulate an increase in the number of moose and caribou for out-of-state hunters.

Deer are largely matriarchal. The older females—the does—teach the young deer important information on habitat and other behavioral knowledge. Hunting often eliminates many older deer before they can impart survival and social skills to their succeeding generations.[27]

And the endlessly touted "successful conservation programs" are not always what they appear to be. For instance, one such pro-gram introduces turkeys and exotic species like pheasant to an area, but it often does so at the expense of the local predator popu-lation. Foxes, coyotes, raccoons (who love eggs), and any pet dogs or cats that happen into the area can be poisoned, trapped, or shot. This is done in order to guarantee and enhance the propagation of the "game" species.

Favorable weather and habitat conditions have allowed ducks to bounce back from their dangerously low populations levels of the mid-1980s. Some historically depleted species, such as the American black duck, the Northern pintail, and the sea ducks, however, are still hunted.

Until the 1980s, an estimated 2 to 3 million waterfowl were dying annually from ingesting poisonous lead shotgun ammuni-tion, which had built up in the bottoms of marshes and wetlands. With the adoption of recent restrictions on the use of lead shot, which were strongly opposed by some hunting groups, the prob-lem is expected to diminish.

THE FUTURE OF SPORT HUNTING

As we enter a new millennium, it is clear that we cannot continue to kill and maim animals on the massive scale we have in the past. With the possible exception of a few animals like deer, such killing is simply not sustainable. With the myriad environmental threats facing our wildlife—habitat destruction, acid rain, pesticides and pollution, global warming, ozone layer depletion—we should be doing all we can to preserve animal populations that are under pressure, not subject them to additional dangers.

But we should not stop hunting animals solely because their numbers are dwindling. Hunting and shooting defenseless animals is an aggressive and odious act of cruelty. We cannot build a humane society on a foundation that sanctions killing as a form of recreation. Animals should not be treated as just a collection of marketable resources or cash crops. They are feeling, sentient creatures that should be spared our slings and arrows, our nets and harpoons, and our guns and greed. The HSUS believes that of the 94 percent of the nonhunting public, most agree with this belief. A 1993 nationwide poll by *The Los Angeles Times* found that 54 percent of Americans "oppose the hunting of animals for sport." Most cases in which The Humane Society of the United States has been able to put hunting issues on state ballots as initiatives, it has won, despite being hugely outspent by the gun lobby.[28]

In recent years, HSUS has succeeded in helping enact laws that ban certain especially cruel hunting practices. For example, it was able to end such practices as bear baiting and hound hunting of bears, mountain lions, bobcats, and lynx in the state of Washington; same-day airborne shooting of wolves and other predators in Alaska; hound hunting of bears and bobcats in Massachusetts; hunting of bears in Colorado with bait and dogs, as well as bear hunting there in the spring and summer, when mothers are still with their cubs.

HSUS senior vice president Wayne Pacelle was instrumental in helping lead and organize support for these ballot initiatives. He believes that we have little choice but to go directly to the people via the ballot box, since state fish and game agencies and wildlife departments are dominated by hunting interests. And the Department of the Interior and its Fish and Wildlife Service ardently promote hunting, even at national wildlife refuges, which are funded by general tax revenues.

The Twilight of the Hunter

The future of hunting will be determined by our nation's young people. Fortunately, they are rejecting the recreational killing of animals in increasingly large numbers. Since 1975, fewer and fewer young people are showing interest in the sport.

According to two leading experts on the demographics of hunting, T.A. Heberlein and E.J. Thomas of the University of Wisconsin, "It is not out of the question that there will be no sport hunting, or a dramatic change in the character of sport hunting, in the United States by mid-century."[29] Three prohunting researchers at Cornell University's Department of Natural Resources—Daniel Decker, Jody Enck, and Tommy Brown—report that "the future of hunting looks bleak given prevailing social values coupled with recent projected trends in American demographics . . . Nearly every published report of hunting trends indicates that the number of participants has declined during the decade of the 1980s and forecasts continued decline into the future."[30]

The hunting lobby is aware of and extremely concerned about the diminishing interest in hunting. Its own studies foresee the end of hunting within sixty years unless it is able to reverse the trend, which it is trying desperately to do. One way it does this is by using taxpayers' money to fund prohunting education and propaganda.[31] Despite all of its efforts to prop up a dying tradition, the Force does not appear to be with the hunting lobby. According to John Atwood, editor of the 113-year-old *Sports Afield*—one of the nation's major hunting and fishing magazines—the publication has recently changed its gunning focus from "blood and guts, rack 'em and sack 'em" to "clay and sport shooting." Indeed, the entire magazine is changing its direction from guns and hunting to more challenging outdoor sports, such as kayaking and rock climbing, which appeal to young people.[32]

Atwood also stated that "the readership of *Sports Afield* was getting on in years." Undoubtedly, this statement was based on Mediamark Research Inc.'s finding that between 1990 and 1998 adult participation in hunting dropped 17 percent, while rock climbing rose 44 percent and backpacking 34 percent. Clearly, for firms that depend on people who enjoy the outdoors, the writing is on the wall.

In its July 6, 1999 issue, *The Wall Street Journal* ran an article commenting on the *Sports Afield* switchover. The article, entitled "Venerable Hunting Magazine Disarms," trumpets the story, and goes on to observe that these days, "Real men don't shoot guns, fool around with bows and arrows, or hunt deer."[33]

Fighting for Children's Hearts and Minds

Another major obstacle facing the hunting industry is the fact that people must be taught to hunt at an early age or they probably never will. As the Fund for Animals points out in its recent landmark report, "Killing Their Childhood: How Public Schools and Government Agencies Are Promoting Sport Hunting to America's Children," the hunting establishment is determined to turn our children into hunters before they develop an aversion to killing and maiming animals:

> Here is the central truth that the hunting industry and the wildlife agencies have run up against in their struggle to recruit new hunters. Men and women who do not become hunters by the time they graduate from high school are unlikely ever to become hunters. . . . Many people choose not to hunt because they find killing animals for recreation offensive. If most people are not desensitized to the suffering and death of animals at an early age, their consciences will never let them hunt.[34]

In light of this, the Fund's study reports that federal and state wildlife agencies "have taken the challenge seriously. They are applying their creativity and energy, they are spending the big money, and they are making the big time commitments. There is now a national campaign underway to recruit children into sport hunting and to neutralize public opposition to hunting."

One way in which wildlife agencies try to desensitize children toward the killing of animals is by sponsoring special children's hunts. This practice literally turns kids into killers. Some participants are as young as eight years old, and several states having no minimum age requirement at all! Florida sponsored the first children's hunt in 1985, and by 1997, forty-two states had jumped on the bandwagon. For children from families who do not hunt, some states offer "mentor programs" that match kids with hunters who teach them the basics, including overcoming their natural aversion to harming animals. Interestingly, the hunts rarely mention the word "children" at all. They are called youth hunts, junior hunts, or, best of all, special hunting opportunities for young people.

"Hunter education" is another euphemism for the recruitment of new, youthful hunters. Programs often use taxpayer money to teach children the importance of "wildlife management" and how to debate animal protectionists. Public school classrooms in many states are being used to preach the virtues of hunting to impressionable youngsters. The United States Fish and Wildlife Service even provided $330,000 of federal Pittman-Robertson funds to the National Shooting Sports Foundation to promote prohunting videos and other materials in public schools throughout the nation.[35]

Someday, the sport itself will die out, much to the benefit not just of the animals, but to ourselves as well. Ultimately, the hunters' efforts will be in vain. According to Dr. John Grandy, Susan Hagood, and Dale Bartlett—members of HSUS's wildlife staff—in *Learn the Facts About Hunting:*

> As a growing body of research has revealed a disturbing link between violence directed at people, and cruelty to animals, society must look critically at the violence and cruelty to wildlife that this country permits, encourages, and even glorifies as recreation. . . . For the well-being of humankind, the animals with whom we share the planet, and the earth itself, now and in the new millennium, we must begin to foster a kinder, gentler, more humane ethic.

We can accomplish this, they conclude, "by ensuring that a clear and consistent respect for life permeates all of our endeavors, and ending once and for all the widespread acceptance of recreational killing of animals."[36]

5. Trapping—Legalized Torture of Animals

It is difficult to think of a widely practiced, government-sanctioned, taxpayer-subsidized activity that is more cruel and less sporting than sport hunting. But trapping is all of these things, and really amounts to legalized maiming and torture of animals for fun and profit.

Trapping has long been attacked by animal protectionists as excessively cruel, wasteful, and destructive to animal populations. But many wildlife and government officials strongly defend it as a necessity for controlling certain species of wildlife, especially predators. State and federal officials actively promote trapping as worthwhile outdoor recreation, especially suitable for youngsters to participate in and enjoy.

The fact is, most of the traps used today are among the most barbaric devices imaginable—vestiges of the Dark Ages. But many animal activist groups are working constantly to see that they are eliminated. And they will not rest until that day comes.

THE CRUELTY OF TRAPPING

Several million animals are trapped in the United States each year. The demand for fur generated by consumers encourages the trapping of millions of additional animals throughout the world.

Most of these animals are taken in steel-jaw leghold traps,

whose spring-powered "jaws" slam shut on the leg or foot of the unfortunate animal that steps in it. The shock and pain an animal first feels when it is caught in a trap must be similar to what we experience when our fingers are slammed in a car door. Now imagine not being able to free them for days or even weeks! Often, a trapped animal will languish for days at a time before dying of thirst, starvation, exposure, blood loss, attack by another animal, or a blow or bullet from a trapper. Animals have even been known to break off their teeth trying to chew through the tough, cold steel of the trap in a desperate effort to get free.[1, 2]

It is not unusual for an animal to free itself by chewing off its trapped leg, especially if it has a mate or young to be fed back at the den. This phenomenon is so common that the trappers actually have a term for it. It's called a "wring-off." Many a trapper has discovered the foot of a raccoon, muskrat, or other creature that crippled itself in an effort to escape the pain, terror, and desperation of the trap.

Those who are most aware of the cruelty of the leghold trap are, of course, the trappers themselves. They still use a device that is essentially unimproved from and operates in a similar way as those that were first imported from Europe three centuries ago. The trap remains popular because it is cheap, maintenance-free, and rarely harms the valuable pelt of the animal.

The suffering caused by these traps is nothing new. Humanitarians have opposed trap usage for many years. In 1863, Charles Darwin wrote an appeal against such traps, saying:

> Few men could endure to watch an animal struggling in a trap with a crushed and torn limb; yet, on all the well-preserved estates throughout the kingdom, animals thus linger every night. . . . It is scarcely possible to exaggerate the suffering thus endured from fear, from acute pain, maddened by thirst, and by vain attempts to escape.[3]

Almost 100 years later, British Prime Minister Winston Churchill called the devices barbaric and worked successfully to have them banned in the British Isles.[4]

WASTEFUL SLAUGHTER

Because of their indiscriminate nature, traps frequently take the lives of nontarget animals—animals for whom the traps were not intended. Over 900 veterinarians responded to a 1986 survey conducted by the Animal Welfare Institute, confirming that huge numbers of nontarget animals are killed in traps. These animals included pet dogs and cats, bald and golden eagles, owls, hawks, colts, lambs, fawns, calves, goats, ducks, and geese. Of the veterinarians who responded to the survey, 76 percent expressed opposition to such traps.[5] Worst of all, children have been victims as well. In some cases, they have been maimed, crippled, or have sustained severe damage to limbs.[6]

Although a skilled and experienced trapper knows where and how to set his traps for the best chance of catching the intended prey, the trap itself is indiscriminate. It is even said that the skeletons of Indians have been found in large bear traps in remote areas of the West. Some early settlers and ranchers would not venture into the wilderness without the proper tools to take apart such a device in case they were accidentally caught in one.[7]

Large traps are no longer legal in most states, but smaller, non-selective traps are still used throughout the country. A thirty-year study conducted by the Denver Wildlife Research Center found that of 1,199 reported animals caught in traps, only 138 were actually targeted by trappers—88.5 percent were nontarget species. These animals—targeted or not—either die or sustain extensive injuries, including broken bones and teeth, and severed tendons and ligaments. Gangrene of a damaged leg can begin within thirty minutes of injury.[8]

A number of states have tightened their regulations on trapping to curtail the accidental harm to pets, livestock, and protected species. The problem is that enforcement of these regulations is practically nonexistent. When a trap is set out in a field or wooded area, it is going to catch whatever creature happens along. Often it is an animal like Cindy, a lost dog who was caught in one of the newer, supposedly humane "padded" steel traps. As recounted in an October 22, 1995, article that appeared in *The Boston Globe:*

> Cindy had been caught in the trap for at least four days, miles deep in the woods of Fall River, before somebody heard her cries. When Joy Bannister, the city's dog officer, found her, the 50-pound hunting dog had leghold traps on both back paws and one of her front legs. The trap on her leg was staked, keeping her from hobbling for help.

"She was chewing off her paw to try to break free from the traps," Bannister says. "She was crying as she did it from the pain. The traps on Cindy's back paws were padded, but they crushed all her toes." Bannister carried her out of the woods, but the injuries to her leg and paws would have required amputations. She was put to sleep.[9]

Ironically, the use of steel leghold traps had been illegal in Massachusetts since 1963, but in June 1995, the state's highest court ruled that soft-catch or padded traps could be used on one's own land, and on any public land.[10]

EARLY AND MODERN-DAY TRAPPING

Trapping animals has a long and important history in the record of human development. It was one of the first ways in which early humans were able to feed and clothe themselves. It is a practice that played a historic role in the settling of North America.

Canada was virtually founded by the fur trade, and the beaver remains its national symbol. This animal also appears in the official seal of New York City, a tribute to the importance of beaver fur to the development of Manhattan Island. For many years, the economy of the northern states was based on beaver skins, which were used much like currency. A blanket was worth six skins; a rifle, twelve. Many eighteenth- and nineteenth-century pioneers made a living trapping beavers, many of which were made into hats for the European market. As a result of the huge demand for their skins, the beaver was nearly wiped out.[11, 12]

The Lewis and Clark expedition of 1804 to 1806 is generally portrayed as a search for the best route to the Pacific Ocean. But it was at the behest of President Thomas Jefferson that Congress funded the trip with the hope of wresting the lucrative fur trade from the British.[13]

More recently, just one 1950s Walt Disney movie that was later turned into a prime-time television show—*Davy Crockett, King of the Wild Frontier*—surely caused the deaths of millions of raccoons, mainly by trapping. This was to satisfy the demand from youngsters for coonskin caps, just like the one worn by this television hero. Now, the mythic trapper is gone, and the "sport" is largely in disrepute.

A recent front-page story in the June 28, 1999 issue of *The Wall Street Journal* called trapping "a calling most love to hate." It stated that "as jobs go, trapping is one lots of Americans love to loathe." The article also stated:

> Through much of the 20th century, trappers like Kit Carson were romanticized in fiction and film with other frontier heroes. But by the end of the 20th century, in a profound twist in public perception, they have been reduced to cruel villains who torture and kill cute little animals.[14]

Today, most trapping is not done for survival. Rather, it is for "sport," hobby, or for supplemental income by a small and diminishing number of people. Trappers in the United States kill several million furbearing animals each year (4 million in 1998; 2.5 million in 1999), with 1.5 million more trapped in Canada. Mainly, these animals include beavers, foxes, minks, muskrats, martens, otters, raccoons, and nutria. (Many minks and foxes are also ranch-raised under horrid conditions for the fur industry.)[15]

Not long ago, there were large numbers of amateur and part-time trappers, especially when pelts of furbearers were bringing high prices. Fortunately, this number has declined greatly in recent years along with the price of pelts. According to the Department of Commerce, as of the mid 1990s, the number of people in the United States who hunt or trap for a living is estimated at only about 2,100, and 86 percent are under the age of twenty.[16]

Based on the licenses sold, there were about 500,000 sport and commercial trappers in the United States in the 1950s and 1960s. In 1988 that figure had dropped significantly to about 338,000. By 1994, it had dropped by more than half to 157,614. The overwhelming majority of licenses were sold to recreational trappers, who supplement their income by selling pelts. But financial incentives are disappearing—a fox pelt that would have brought a trapper eighty dollars in the late 1970s is now worth only about sixteen dollars.[17, 18, 19]

THE THREAT TO WILDLIFE SURVIVAL

Trappers claim that their activities are useful and even necessary in ensuring a natural balance of wildlife. Proponents of trapping frequently voice the theme that wildlife is a natural resource to be used and "managed," and that trappers, by "harvesting" surplus animals, are living in harmony with nature. They argue that humans are part of nature and its cycles, and that trapping helps maintain nature's balance by managing populations of animals that would otherwise be "controlled" by even harsher methods, such as starvation and disease.

There is no real evidence to support this theory, so let's just call it what it is—propaganda. In fact, some species have been so intensively trapped that they have become rare, endangered, or totally eliminated from numerous areas. Species that are currently threatened by trapping, at least in part, include the river otter, fisher, Canadian lynx, and bobcat.

Some animals that are legally trapped in the United States are known to be threatened with extinction or vulnerable to becoming so. States that allow trapping of bobcats, lynx, gray wolves, mountain lions, and river otters must, under international law, require that tags be attached to the pelts of these animals. This is done because they are listed by an international wildlife protection treaty—the Convention on International Trade in Endangered Species of Wild Flora and Fauna (CITES)—as threatened or likely to become so if heavily traded.

SNARING WOLVES IN ALASKA

In recent years, the state of Alaska has tried to drastically reduce its wolf population in certain areas in order to increase "hunting opportunities" for moose and caribou, which are a source of food for wolves. However, when hunting these animals for food, wolves instinctively take the weak, sick, diseased, very young, or very old ones, perpetuating that timeless truism of nature, "survival of the fittest." Therefore, reducing the number of wolves does not necessarily translate into more moose and caribou and certainly not into healthier ones![20]

Nevertheless, Alaska is determined to get rid of many of its wolves. It is the last place in the United States with the exception of Minnesota where a large and viable wolf population exists. Since a 1996 ballot initiative effectively eliminated airplane-assisted land-and-shoot wolf killing, the state Department of Fish and Game turned to a particularly brutal trapping technique known as saturation snaring, and has enthusiastically promoted this method to local "sportsmen" and trappers.

The trap itself is a simple snare made of tough, thin wire that tightens around the leg, paw, or snout of any animal that becomes ensnared, eventually penetrating through the animal's flesh and into bone, causing a slow, painful, and terrifying death. The snares are cheap, costing less than a dollar apiece, and dozens can easily be placed on trees and bushes of trails used by animals. Each year, half of the wolves killed in Alaska die in snares, as do many non-target animals such as caribou, moose, and even eagles.[21]

THE FUR INDUSTRY

Traditionally, the American and international fur industries have provided the major incentive for the trapping of animals. But in recent years, as fur has become less fashionable and more controversial, fur sales have declined, and with it, the trapping of fur-bearers.

Increasing Public Awareness

Indeed, largely as a result of public awareness campaigns by animal protection groups, increasingly large numbers of people have opened their eyes to the cruelty behind fur coats. In recent years, they have stayed away from them in droves. Because of this, tens of millions of animals have been spared torture and death, just in the United States alone! In Danielle Bays' 1998 article, "Is Fur Really Back?" she states, "Since the late 1980s, the fur industry has been in a free fall. The number of U.S. fur manufacturers and retailers has been cut in half, and those that remain are struggling to survive. Macy's West stores have even closed their fur departments."[22]

American trappers have been bolstered somewhat by the European market, which imports 80 percent of the pelts taken in the United States. Even in Europe, however, the demand for fur has fallen dramatically as public sentiment, particularly among young people, has shifted against wearing it.

Despite advertising campaigns proclaiming that "Fur is Back!" the industry is well aware that its ship is sinking. Recent public opinion polls show that up to 74 percent of Americans oppose fur as fashion. In 1998, a columnist for the industry publication *Fur*

World wrote, "Let's face it, fur has an image problem. It's no longer the 'must have' item in a woman's wardrobe, despite all the rhetoric to the contrary." Those who strive for a humane society enthusiastically agree.[23, 24]

According to Patricia Forkan—executive vice president of The HSUS—fur items, rather than being flaunted, often are now so downplayed in garments that they are hardly noticed: "Some of the fur fashion being designed today, you wouldn't even recognize as being part of an animal. It has been sheared, dyed, even knitted to look more like an inoffensive fabric. Today's women don't want to look like they live in a cave."[25] This bad news for the fur industry is certainly good news for animals.

In addition to the decrease in the number of animals being trapped each year, fur-farm operations have also declined. Since the 1980s, the number of these farms has dropped by more than half, and the "ranched" mink who are killed for their fur has fallen by at least 35 percent.[26, 27]

The Fur Industry's Ugly Secret

In 1998, The HSUS concluded an eighteen-month-long undercover investigation that dealt a devastating public relations blow to the fur industry. It revealed the industry's ugly little secret—the cruel slaughter of dogs and cats for the fur trade.

When this scandal was given prominent coverage on *Dateline NBC*, as well as network evening news shows and major newspapers, it had a profound effect on the public. There is something uniquely horrifying about the cruel trade in animals that could be our own pets. Imagine, for example, how the investigators felt upon seeing dogs who were about to be killed, still wagging their tails, still showing trust in humans. As one of the investigators put it, "Looking at these animals, I couldn't help thinking about the enormous trust that dogs and cats place in people. The magnitude of the betrayal of that trust that we witnessed was truly beyond belief, and all to satisfy a selfish desire for fur."[28]

During HSUS' investigative research, which was conducted jointly with Humane Society International (HSI) and German Journalist Manfred Karremann, investigators met with those who kept and brutally killed dogs and cats. They also met with the sellers, buyers, manufacturers, retailers, and middlemen in Asia and Europe.

Richard W. Swain, Jr., HSUS vice president for investigations, has described how his undercover team saw piles of cat pelts of every color and the skins of German shepherds and mixed-breed dogs—adults and puppies alike. Many had been pets who were lost or stolen. It is particularly shocking that most of these dogs who are bred and killed for their fur are German shepherds, the same courageous and noble breed that leads the blind, rescues victims of disasters, and patrols our streets in partnership with police officers across the land.

While touring a Chinese warehouse, the investigators saw piles of skins that were soon-to-be "fun furs." Among them, they saw what appeared to be golden retriever pelts, which were on sale for fourteen dollars apiece, and a fur "plate" that consisted of skins from the heads of thirty-six gray tabby cats that were sewn together. They were priced at fifteen dollars. All of these creatures had died agonizing deaths. They had been strangled, drowned, or skinned alive.

At a local butcher shop, they saw "half a dozen dogs of varying breeds, tethered by thin metal wires, shivering in the darkness. Above them, the bodies of skinned dogs hang from hooks in the ceiling. The silence is eerie; there is no sound except for the quiet whimpering of a puppy lying on the frozen ground."

At a slaughterhouse in Thailand, investigators watched as a fresh shipment of "furs-to-be" arrived for processing: "One dog after another, howling in pain, is pulled from the truck by means of a wire noose attached to a wooden catchpole. A black mixed-breed pup watches in terror as his companions are brutally slaughtered. A heart-shaped pendant with the word 'love' hangs from the collar around his neck."

United States law does not ban the importing of dog or cat pelts into the country, and amendments to the Fur Products Labeling Act exempt labeling requirements on most fur-trimmed garments, specifically those costing less than $150. The investigators were told by the exporters that they would place any label the customer wanted on the garment, effectively disguising the type of animal used. Thus, the only sure way to avoid cat or dog fur on imported clothing is not to buy any product made from real fur.

Even an accurate label does not necessarily prevent dog and cat fur from being sold in the United States. Recently, at the Burlington Coat Factory, HSUS investigators discovered jackets

trimmed with what was labeled "Mongolia dog fur." Upon learning of this, Burlington quickly pulled the coats from its over 250
stores. Since then, it has actively worked to ban further imports.

As Patricia Forkan points out, this investigation shone a light
into the deepest, darkest, innermost depths of the fur industry.
It revealed its true nature, unfiltered by glamorous models and
expensive publicity campaigns:

> Those who make money from the fur industry or buy fur
> products may truly think that traditional furbearing ani-
> mals are somehow less capable of suffering. That illusion
> should be shattered when they're faced with the horrors of
> the dog and cat fur trade. . . . Fur is a product that can exist
> only through the suffering and death of millions of ani-
> mals. Dogs and cats are merely the victims most of us know
> the best and love the most.[29]

The findings of this investigation were upsetting indeed; however, they did result in somewhat of a happy ending. The revela-
tions widely reported in the news media around the Christmas
season of 1998 further discredited furs in the eyes of millions of people. And as for that little black puppy with the heart-shaped pendant on his collar—he was rescued and placed in a loving home.

TRAPPING TO CONTROL PREDATORS

Interestingly, the biggest wildlife trapper in America is the United
States government. It uses our tax dollars to kill, mostly through
trapping, a reported 100,000 wild animals each year in the western
states. This is done mainly to protect sheep and cattle from predators.

The Government's Role

Every year, the Department of Agriculture's Animal Damage Control (ADC) Program uses between 20,000 to 30,000 traps, and
approximately $30 million dollars, to trap, shoot, poison, and burn
some 100,000 predators along with their pups and cubs. A typical
reported annual death toll includes approximately 85,000 coyotes,
9,000 foxes, 2,000 bobcats, 300 mountain lions, 160 black bears, plus
an assortment of nontarget animals such as eagles, livestock, and
family pets.[30]

Even in the eastern United States where predators are far less abundant, predator control devastates innocent animal populations. A study funded by the ADC on coyote trapping in New York State found that the predator control program there caught as many as eleven nontarget animals for every coyote killed.[31]

Much of this slaughter takes place on federal publicly owned western rangelands that are leased to livestock ranchers at giveaway prices—often just pennies an acre. The below-market leasing fees as well as free "predator control" and other services provided by the taxpayers have led many conservationists to refer to wealthy cattle and sheep raisers as "welfare ranchers," which is exactly what they are.[32]

It is true that the government's large-scale trapping program is not nearly as ecologically devastating as the use of poison. Once used on a widespread scale, poison bait, now greatly restricted, was a much more indiscriminate and destructive "control" method. But biologists point out that the massive persecution of coyotes has resulted in female coyotes producing larger litters of pups at an earlier age, while at the same time breaking up their social and family structure. The result is continual escalation in livestock losses to coyotes. Many if not most of the predators taken are not livestock killers.[33]

If trapping furbearers can no longer provide a living, killing predators can. For example, John Graham, a predator control trapper in eastern Montana, used 500 traps and 1,800 snares to bag over 500 coyotes, 350 red foxes, 43 bobcats, and numerous badgers, raccoons, and skunks in the 1998–1999 winter season. While he makes less than $10,000 a year selling his pelts (he gets about $13 for a red fox, $20 to $25 for a coyote, and about $150 for a bobcat), local ranchers pay him $39,000 to control the population of predators. His trapping, he believes, also increases the numbers of deer, antelope, elk, exotic grouse, and pheasants, which bring in more hunters with money to spend on guides, outfitters, and local businesses.[34]

The Value of Predators

Despite all of the rhetoric to the contrary, killing predators, such as coyotes, on a large scale upsets rather than maintains nature's balance. It eliminates valuable animals that prey mainly on rabbits, mice, rats, and other creatures that are known to harm crops and spread diseases that threaten humans.

For example, in the spring of 1998, the southwestern United States experienced extraordinarily high levels of rainfall caused by the El Niño weather phenomenon. This, in turn, stimulated the explosive growth of new vegetation in the deserts of New Mexico, Arizona, Colorado, and other areas. The vegetation provided abundant food sources for rodents like deer mice, which carry the deadly hantavirus pulmonary syndrome. Hantavirus can and does kill people.

By the summer of 1998, there was a surging population of deer mice (twenty times that of the previous year). The numbers were fast approaching those of 1993, the year that an outbreak of hantavirus killed 28 people in the southwest. By June of 1999, there were 217 people in thirty states who had become infected with the rodent-borne virus. Of these, 94 had died. In the southwestern states, residents began buying housecats to help eliminate any mice.[35, 36, 37] If only the coyotes and other predators had been left alone, perhaps they could have prevented many cases of hantavirus. By hunting and eating mice and other rodents, they would have helped keep their populations in check. Theoretically, every coyote killed means more deer mice to live, reproduce, and continue to threaten humans.

We should be protecting coyotes and other predators who could help reduce the incidence of hantavirus. Their control of deer mice is free, effective, and sensible, and it can help avert public health crises. A moratorium on the nonemergency killing of predators should be in effect, especially in those areas affected by hantavirus. Those living in the southwestern United States should consider that sparing coyotes might save their lives.

FIGHTING TO BAN TRAPPING

In recent decades, opposition to trapping—particularly the use of steel-jaw, leghold traps—has mounted. Animal protection groups such as The Humane Society of the United States, the Animal Welfare Institute, Friends of Animals, and The Fund for Animals have launched vigorous campaigns to ban or restrict trapping and to discourage the buying and wearing of fur. Their efforts have begun to pay off.

Eighty-eight countries worldwide have banned steel-jaw, leghold traps on the grounds that they are inordinately cruel and nonselective. Norway was the first country to ban them, followed by the United Kingdom, which eliminated the devices, called gin traps, between 1959 and 1965.[38, 39, 40] In 1991, the fifteen-nation European Union (EU) agreed to prohibit the use of these traps beginning in 1995. It also restricted fur imports from nations where the traps are still used (including the United States). But the ban was never implemented due to opposition from the United States and Canada, which threatened, among other things, to take the case to the World Trade Organization.[41, 42]

Efforts in the United States to ban the trap through national legislation have not succeeded, despite public opinion polls showing strong support for such a measure. A 1978 survey found that 78 percent of the public was opposed to the traps; a December 1996 poll showed that 74 percent of Americans believed that the traps should be banned outright.[43, 44] The American Veterinary Medical Association, the World Veterinary Association, and the American Animal Hospital Association have all condemned leghold traps as "inhumane."[45]

During the 1992 presidential campaign, Bill Clinton went on record as opposing any cruelty to animals. As a senator, Vice President Al Gore co-sponsored a bill to ban leghold traps. Unfortunately, the Clinton-Gore Administration never acted to restrict trapping, and actually made the situation worse. It was during this administration that the United States and Canada lobbied vigorously and successfully to prevent the European Union from banning the import of fur pelts from nations still using the trap. They pressured the EU by combining a variety of economic threats as well as incentives.[46, 47, 48, 49]

Efforts to restrict trapping have also been effectively opposed by a coalition of trappers and trap manufacturers, the fur industry, and state and federal wildlife officials. Opposition has also come from pro-wildlife "management" lobbying groups such as The National Rifle Association, The Wildlife Legislative Fund of America, The International Association of Fish and Wildlife Agencies, and The National Trappers Association. Animal protectionists have found more success at the state level, where, in about twenty states, issues are able to be placed on ballots. A number of states, including New Jersey, Colorado, Massachusetts, Rhode Island, Florida, and Arizona have passed laws restricting the sale, manufacture, and/or use of leghold traps. Most of these laws allow for their use under certain circumstances, such as to protect public health and safety.[50, 51, 52]

Most state laws regulating trapping remain woefully inadequate. Twenty-nine states allow the use of traps with teeth, which rip the flesh of an animal as it struggles to free itself. Only sixteen states require that traps be checked every twenty-four hours. Other states allow two to three days between visits. Four states—Alaska, Michigan, Montana, and North Dakota—have no checking requirements at all. The worst part is that no matter what regulations may be in place, they are virtually impossible to enforce in any meaningful way.[53]

Ironically, even when animal protectionists lose a ballot initiative, progress is made in educating the public. For instance, in 1999 in Beverly Hills, California, home to some of the most posh and expensive fur salons anywhere in the world, there was an attempt to get a truth-in-labeling ballot initiative. This would have required all furs and trim to bear a tag stating: "This product is made with fur from animals that may have been killed by electrocution, gassing, stomping, or drowning and may have been trapped in steel-jaw, leghold traps."

Although the initiative was defeated following an expensive campaign by the fur industry, the massive publicity generated by the effort opened the eyes of huge numbers of people to the real ways in which pelts are procured for furriers.

INFLUENCE FROM THE FASHION WORLD

As the fur industry dies, inevitably, sport and commercial trapping will also. One cannot exist without the other, and the majority of Americans entering the twenty-first century clearly prefer live animals to dead furs. Yes, furs are dead—even the most fashion-conscious Americans won't wear them.

No one understands this new attitude better than the vicar of the fashion world, renowned designer Oleg Cassini. "Long, long ago," he regretfully recalled in a recent interview, "I did a coat for [First Lady] Jackie Kennedy. I suggested a leopard coat to her. She loved the idea. . . . It was a success in the fashion world, an instant success. But it had a horrendous result on the world of leopards. The result was that [thousands of] leopards were killed worldwide."[54]

A decade later, having been devastated in large part by the demands of the fur industry, the leopard was placed on the Department of the Interior's list of endangered species, along with the cheetah, ocelot, tiger, snow leopard, jaguar, margay, and tiger cat. Furs had certainly become "hot" fashion items. Between 1968 and 1970, the United States fur industry imported 18,456 leopard skins, 31,105 jaguar pelts, and an incredible 349,680 ocelot skins. It also imported over 3,000 cheetah pelts, representing one-and-a-half times the estimated number of cheetahs remaining in all of the parks in Africa in 1972.[55, 56]

Today, Oleg Cassini designs an upscale collection of fake furs, or, as he calls the imitation fabrics, "Evolutionary Fur—an elegant, stylish substitute" that will be "a frontal attack" on the fur industry.[57] His transformation came about, he says, after "I began to read articles. I began to look at the pictures, to see the frightening cruelty. . . . Anyone who is familiar with animals . . . knows the animals suffer. Animals sense when they're about to be killed. They have the imagination to fear. They cry . . . "

Oleg Cassini believes that the fur industry "will eventually die" as the profit incentive shifts away from real animal fur. He also believes that it will not go quietly: "Its just pure money. . . . And today we're seeing its last defense, the rearguard defense of people who just want to make money . . . who for gain will do anything and camouflage it with lofty ideas and words."[58]

HOPE IN THE NEW MILLENNIUM

As the new millennium begins, The HSUS hopes to help put the fur industry out of its misery with its "Fur-Free 2000" campaign. This crusade urges people to "Have a Fur-Free Holiday," and "Be Fur-Free in the New Century." Among the celebrities joining this campaign are television talk show host Bill Maher, cartoonist Berkeley Breathed, and actors Angela Basset, Betty White, Jack Lemmon, and Diane Keaton.

The basic mission of the campaign is to urge people to go fur-free. You can get involved by taking the following actions:

❑ Refuse to buy or wear any clothing or toys made or trimmed with fur, and don't shop at stores that sell such items. Be sure to inform the store manager of your feelings and write a letter to the company president as well.

❏ Get your friends and family involved; tell them the truth about fur.

❏ If you have a fur and will no longer wear it, donate it to a wildlife rehabilitator. The fur will be used to comfort orphaned and injured animals.

❏ Write letters to the editors of your newspapers, as well as to your state and federal legislators, urging them to work to ban trapping.[59]

Above all, set an example. Be part of the solution. Speak out on the issue, and spread the word. Ask people, "How can a coat made from animals that suffered and died be beautiful?" Remind them that it takes from thirty to sixty minks to make a fur coat, but only one consumer to make a difference.[60]

6. SPECIES EXTINCTION AND THE THREAT TO HUMANITY

In the perhaps 1.5 trillion days since the earth was born and began producing and evolving the myriad marvelous species alive today, a wondrous Creation has emerged. But in the blink of an eye, historically speaking, in just a few short decades, we have greatly diminished this biological diversity, and have destroyed many of the planet's unique life forms. Even worse, we are on the verge of extirpating many, many more.[1] In the words of Harvard Professor Edward O. Wilson, "Many of the earth's vital resources are about to be exhausted. . . . We are dismantling a support system that is too complex to understand, let alone replace . . ."[2]

Much of the fabric of life on earth seems to be unraveling, and we are losing an array of life forms that may provide the foundation for the planet's ability to nurture and sustain life. This is a great catastrophe. It could have profound and irreversible consequences for human civilization: the permanent destruction of millions of unique, valuable, and irreplaceable species of plants and animals that provide us with a variety of vital services. These gifts of nature are potentially invaluable as future sources of food, drugs, and medicines. We are not even aware of the existence of most of these species, let alone their biological importance.

THE HISTORY OF MASS EXTINCTIONS

There is nothing new about species becoming extinct. In fact, it is thought that some 99.9 percent of the billions of species that have evolved have also been lost during the earth's 3.5 to 4 billion years. What makes our modern era unique is the rapidity with which life forms are being lost. In the history of the planet, there has never been a period when so many species were disappearing as quickly as they are today.[3, 4]

Mass extinctions on earth seem to occur every 50 million years or so, give or take a few million. Five mass extinction episodes have been identified since life appeared on the earth. The largest known cataclysm came some 250 million years ago at the end of the Permian period, when a huge die-off of species may have eliminated up to 96 percent of the life forms. The most recent mass extinction occurred some 65 million years ago at the end of the Cretaceous period, when the dinosaurs and many creatures of the ocean disappeared.[5, 6, 7]

Most prehistoric extinctions occurred gradually over thousands or millions of years, and were caused by changes in climate and habitat, loss of food sources, volcanic eruptions, and even meteors or asteroids that struck the earth. By contrast, much of today's rapid and mass extinction of plants and animals is the result of direct human action. Consider how the tropical rain forests, coral reefs, and other biologically rich areas, teeming with life, are destroyed or altered. Currently, the rate of extinction is estimated to be 100 to 1,000 times the natural level.

LOSING 50,000 SPECIES A YEAR

No one really knows how many species of plants and animals are lost every year. Many disappearing organisms have never even been discovered by scientists or seen by humans, much less studied. But estimates by knowledgeable experts are staggering.

Published projections indicate that species extinctions may be taking place several times an hour! In *Keeping Options Alive*—published by the World Resources Institute, and based upon an exhaustively researched and documented 1989 study—authors Walter V. Reid and Kenton R. Miller warn the public "if current trends continue, roughly 5 to 10 percent of the world's species will be lost per decade over the next quarter century." They calculate "between 1990 and 2020, species extinctions caused primarily by tropical deforestation may eliminate somewhere between 5 and 15 percent of the world's species. With roughly 10 million species on earth, this would amount to a potential loss of 15,000 to 50,000 species per year, or 50 to 150 per day."[8]

A twenty-year study conducted by botanists and conservationists around the world was made public in April 1998. Some of the major participants in the study included The New York Botanical Garden, The Nature Conservancy, and The Smithsonian Institution's National Museum of Natural History. It revealed that at least one in eight species of plants worldwide was threatened with extinction. The study added some 34,000 plants to the World Conservation Union's authoritative *IUCN Red List* of species in jeopardy.

Among the most imperiled types of plants were irises and lilies, with 32 percent of all species in danger. The study also concluded that 29 percent of all palms and 14 percent of all rose and cherry species were in danger of extinction as well. It ranked the United States first among all nations in having the greatest number of plants at risk, with 4,669 out of 16,108 species in some danger.[9]

In 1980, *The Global 2000 Report to the President*, prepared jointly by the United States Department of State and the President's Council on Environmental Quality, warned that "between half a million and two million species—15 to 20 percent of all species on earth—could be extinguished by the year 2000." Botanist Peter Raven, Director of the Missouri Botanical Garden, calculated several years ago that by 2010, a quarter of the world's species will have disappeared.[10, 11]

TROPICAL RAIN FORESTS

Probably the most biologically rich areas on earth are the tropical rain forests. It is estimated that anywhere from 50 to 90 percent of the world's plant and animal species live here. As the rain forests are being cut down at a rate of one to two acres a second—the equivalent to twenty football fields a minute—it stands to reason that most extinctions occur here as well.[12]

The biological diversity of the animal kingdom in tropical forests is almost inconceivable. In Peru, one nature preserve harbors more species of birds than are found in the entire United States; half an acre of its rain forest may shelter 40,000 different kinds of insects. A square mile in the lowland part of the country, or in the Amazon area of Brazil or Ecuador, can shelter more than 1,500 types of butterflies, over twice as many as are found in all of Canada and the United States. One Brazilian river can contain more species of fish than are found in all of the rivers of America.[13]

This biological treasure trove, the richest concentration of living things on the planet, is under relentless assault. Vast areas are disappearing every day. And in the words of Harvard Professor Edward O. Wilson, "The loss of genetic and species diversity by the destruction of natural habitats [is] the folly our descendants are least likely to forgive us."

Some recent known rain forest losses include the following: half of the estimated fourteen birds on the island of Cebu in the Philippines, over half of the freshwater fish species of peninsular Asia, and over ninety plant species that had been growing on the ridge of a mountain in Ecuador. The nations of Ecuador, Madagascar, and the Philippines have lost at least two-thirds of their rain forests, and what remains is being cut down rapidly. Every day, new roads are being cut into the virgin rain forests of central Africa. There is hardly a rain forest on earth that is safe from the chainsaw and the hunters that follow in its path.[14]

Probably the best-known class of life forms—the mammals— are also the most endangered, with over two thousand types listed by international authorities as threatened or vulnerable to some extent. As United States Fish and Wildlife Service (FWS) scientists wrote in a May 1997 publication entitled "Noah's Ark is Leaking," up to half of all mammals may be in danger:

> The number of mammals around the world recognized as being in jeopardy by scientific authorities is multiplying, nearly tripling in just the past ten years. These endangered animals constitute nearly a quarter of all the world's full species of mammals. If subspecies are added in, the actual number of mammals in jeopardy is much closer to a half than to a fourth of the world's total.[15]

CHAIN REACTION EXTINCTIONS

In an article in *The Atlanta Constitution* entitled "With every leap, you must prepare a landing," columnist Tom Teepen writes:

> The short story (by Ray Bradbury), as I recollect it, was set in a future where time travel had become possible. A fellow signed up to tour the primeval past and, like others, was cautioned to remain on the floating path and to touch nothing, because even the smallest alteration in the past could have huge consequences. He made the trip and marveled at the exotic plants and creatures of an era beyond reckoning. He scrupulously stayed on the path, but returned to his own time to find everything changed grotesquely, and in no way for the better. Puzzled, he sat down, only to discover, from the evidence on his shoe sole, that in the ancient past he had stepped on a butterfly.[16]

We have been stepping on too many butterflies lately. And the results are already becoming apparent in the tropical forests. Because of the complex and intricate relationship that has evolved between many tropical species, the disappearance or depletion of one can quickly cause the loss of others. As science researcher and writer Erik Eckholm points out in his book *Disappearing Species: The Social Challenge*, the removal of a single plant species from an area can jeopardize ten to thirty other species of insects and other plants. He observes that each of the forty or so fig trees found in Central America has a specific insect pollinator, as well as other insect pollinators that are dependent on many of the trees for food. As Eckholm puts it, "Crushed by the march of civilization, one species can take many others with it, and the ecological repercussion and arrangements that follow may well endanger people."[17]

IMPACT OF MASS EXTINCTIONS

No one can predict what the impact of mass extinctions of species will be, but the course of evolution will certainly be profoundly affected, perhaps disastrously so. "The Global Environment and Basic Human Needs," a 1978 report by the President's Council on Environmental Quality, observes that in the years to come "unique ecosystems populated by thousands of unrecorded plant and animal species face rapid destruction—irreversible genetic losses that will profoundly alter the course of evolution."[18] Writer Erik Eckholm warns that "should this biological massacre take place, evolution will no doubt continue, but in a grossly distorted manner":

> Such a multitude of species losses would constitute a basic and irreversible alteration in the nature of the biosphere even before we can understand its workings—an evolutionary Rubicon whose crossing Homo sapiens would do well to avoid. . . . Humans appoint themselves as the ultimate arbiters of evolution and determine its future course on the basis of short-term considerations and a great deal of ignorance. . . . Scientists cannot yet say where the critical threshholds lie, at what level of species extermination the web of life will be seriously disrupted . . . "[19]

One cannot foresee how disastrous to humanity the loss of so many plant species will be. As John Tuxill points out in the 1999 edition of Worldwatch's *State of the World*, "For all of human history, we have depended on plants and the rest of biodiversity for our soul and subsistence."[20] As the President's Council on Environmental Quality observes in its 1978 report, "Perhaps the greatest industrial, agricultural, and medical costs of species reduction will stem from future opportunities unknowingly lost."[21]

Lost Foods, Drugs, and Medicines

As one species after another disappears, we are losing countless beautiful and interesting life forms that enrich our lives and lift our spirits. But there is a more tangible and dangerous aspect to this loss. From our spaceship earth, we casually toss much of our life support equipment overboard without realizing its function. This is especially true of plants. The *IUCN Red List of Threatened Plants* lists over 33,000 species that are threatened to some extent; 380 are known to be extinct.

As Professor Edward O. Wilson observes in his book *Consilience*, "Each species is a masterpiece of evolution, offering a vast source of useful scientific knowledge because it is so thoroughly adapted to the environment in which it lives." He goes on to say, "Species alive today are thousands to millions years old. Their genes, having been tested by adversity over so many generations, engineer a staggeringly complex array of biochemical devices to aid the survival and reproduction of the organisms carrying them."[22]

In its *World Conservation Strategy Report* of March 1980, the United Nations Environment Program observed that the value of the species being lost is immense if incalculable:

> Penicillin, digitalis, quinine, rubber, pectin, resins, gums, insecticides—these and other medicines and products come from plants. One out of two [or one out of four] prescriptions filled in the U.S. each day is for a drug based on an ingredient in a plant. . . . The wheat we know today began as wild plants, and some humans some unknown number of years ago may well have considered those wild plants worthless weeds.[23]

As the President's Council on Environmental Quality observed in its 1978 report, many potentially useful products and foods are vanishing forever without our ever realizing the loss:

> Only about 5 percent of the world's plant species have yet been screened for pharmacologically active ingredients. Ninety percent of the food that humans eat comes from just twelve crops, but scores of thousands of plants are edible, and some will undoubtedly prove useful in meeting human food needs.[24]

John Tuxill writes of the dependence of humans on plants in Worldwatch's 1999 edition of *State of the World*:

> People everywhere rely on plants for staying healthy and extending the quality and length of their lives. One quarter of the prescription drugs marketed in North America and Europe contain active ingredients derived from plants. Plant-based drugs are part of the standard medical procedures for treating heart conditions, childhood leukemia, lymphatic cancer, glaucoma, and many other serious illnesses. Worldwide, the over-the-counter value of these drugs is estimated at more than $40 billion annually.[25]

In addition, according to the World Health Organization, some 3.5 billion people in developing countries depend on plant-based medicine for their health care.

The tropical forests that are being destroyed so rapidly are the main source for the plants whose ingredients we utilize in many medicines, including three quarters of the drugs used in treating cancer. For instance, the major drug used to treat childhood leukemia is derived from the rosy periwinkle plant, which comes from Madagascar's forests. Even such a widely used drug as aspirin is derived from salicylic acid, which comes from the bark of certain willow trees, such as the American aspen.

Tropical forests have also been the original source of such important foods as rice, millet, bananas, pineapples, citrus fruits, coffee, cassava, sugar cane, cola, yams, various kinds of nuts and peppers, and, most important of all, cocoa!

Other endangered and little-known species whose immense potential value to humans are seldom-appreciated are numerous types of native snails, clams, scuds, and other mollusks and crustaceans. They are in peril as the result of a variety of human activities, including dam building, stream channeling, dredging, and water pollution. As pointed out by Dr. Marc Imlay, former biologist with the Department of the Interior's Office of Endangered Species, these organisms may "seem inconsequential in size, but mussels and crustaceans are an indispensable part of the living world." He states:

> Besides fitting into the food chain, these creatures have recently been recognized as being able to produce poisons, antibiotics, tranquilizers, antispasmodics, and antiseptic chemicals in their systems. Scientists believe that these unique abilities can be used as models for the development of synthetic drugs.

We are eliminating forever numerous life forms that might conceivably provide cures for such dreaded diseases as cancer and HIV/AIDS. They could also be a valuable food source to help feed an increasingly hungry and overcrowded planet. Tragically, we will never even know what we have lost. But as Harvard's Edward O. Wilson observes, "Since we depend on functioning ecosystems to clean our water, enrich our soil, and create the very air we breathe, biodiversity is clearly not something to discard carelessly."[26]

Danger at the Bottom of the Sea

In addition to the threatened species of life on earth, an entire and virtually unknown world of life forms on the floor of the deep ocean may be endangered. As *The New York Times* science writer William J. Broad reported in an article on June 1, 1999, "Hordes of creatures living in the hidden depths of the deep sea are in danger of starving to death. . . . This remote part of the planet is believed to harbor millions of undiscovered species, an unknown number of which may be in crisis." The article goes on to say:

> Possibly because of global warming and the resulting increase in sea surface temperatures, a decline of zooplankton may be causing food shortages for deep sea creatures, a study in the North Pacific Ocean indicates. This puts in peril such organisms as corals, crabs, prawns, sponges, sea urchins, sea cucumbers, sea anemones, snails, slugs, worms, barnacles, brittle stars, feather stars, sea lilies, and various kinds of fish. Scientists estimate that in the depths of the sea may live up to 10 million species, seven times more than the estimated 1.4 million that live on the land.[27]

The world's oceans are responsible for the production of much of our vital food and oxygen, and the absorption of harmful greenhouse gases like carbon dioxide. Since ocean health is essential to the well-being of the planet's life forms, a disruption of this ecosystem could be ominous for the future of our civilization.

THE POLITICS OF WILDLIFE

Certainly, when Bruce Babbitt became Secretary of the Interior, it was apparent that conservation concerns would be high on his agenda. His sensitivity to such issues was made clear in October 1992, in an address to a national conference of The HSUS. At that time, he was serving as the president of The League of Conservation Voters—the national, non-partisan political arm of the environmental movement.

As Secretary of the Interior, Babbitt has been, in many ways, a courageous and effective leader. He has worked hard to preserve America's natural treasures by restoring the Florida Everglades, protecting Yellowstone National Park from a proposed gold mine, creating a national monument to protect the red rock canyons of Utah, and proposing a $1 billion Lands Legacy Initiative to pre-serve other natural areas and to help states and communities save their local green spaces.

Yet, even a secretary who demonstrates such a high level of commitment sometimes has difficulty overcoming the threat of the hunting lobby and other special interest groups, as well as the FWS bureaucracy. In recent years, for example, powerful congressional leaders have tried, with some success, to cripple or even kill the Endangered Species Act. While Secretary Babbitt has worked to negotiate a series of compromises, he has been forced by a largely anti-conservation Congress to adopt an essentially defensive pos-ture on several controversial issues, including the listing of new species.

Surely, sound scientific evidence, not the politics of special interests, should dictate if a species should be listed under the ESA. But an emasculated ESA would be catastrophic for wildlife, as well as for our society. This is the dilemma conservationists face today, and the background to many of the battles over protecting endangered species that are currently taking place.

DOOMING SPECIES IN PERIL

The United States government agency with the prime responsibili-ty for listing and protecting imperiled species is the Department of the Interior's Fish and Wildlife Service (FWS). But under the Clin-ton-Gore Administration and under pressure from the Republican-controlled Congress, this agency has, in many ways, virtually abandoned enforcement of the Endangered Species Act (ESA). It has allowed many species to become further endangered and even extinct.

Some 1,100 species are currently listed as endangered or threat-ened, so they enjoy some protection under the Act. A little over half of these species are found in the United States. But thousands of additional species are also imperiled, and many continue to be hunted or traded by Americans.

In December 1997, a group of federal government employees became so concerned about the situation that it issued a White Paper documenting "the Department of Interior's practice of consistently overruling the recommendations of its own scientists to list species as threatened or endangered under the ESA." The report went on to charge that "this posture is part of a deliberate campaign by the highest officials in the Department to frustrate the implementation of the ESA."[28]

The White Paper, entitled "War of Attrition: Sabotage of the Endangered Species Act by the U.S. Department of the Interior," was published by Public Employees for Environmental Responsibility (PEER). This is a Washington, D.C.-based association of biologists, scientists, conservation and law enforcement officials, and other federal, state, and local government professionals with responsibility for environmental and natural resource issues.

Citing the work of FWS' own biologists, the White Paper describes in detail how the agency has "suspended enforcement of the ESA, systematically refusing to list new species despite the findings of its own scientists." It states:

> Without listing, wildlife are vulnerable to continued habitat destruction, poaching, and trafficking in their parts and products. . . . [but] FWS has ceased review of almost all new listing petitions, yet is spending millions of dollars to fight lawsuits brought by environmental groups to force listings . . . . The listing recommendations of FWS biologists have been reversed by Interior for non-biological reasons, in clear violation of the law. . . ."[29]

Pressured by special interest groups, the FWS has turned its back on a number of species in dire need of protection. It has dragged its feet in listing threatened species such as the Canada lynx and the North American bighorn sheep, while expediting the removal or *de-listing* of other species such as the American bald eagle.

Wiping Out the Lynx

The case of the Canada lynx is one example of how special interests have succeeded in pressuring the FWS to deny protection to vanishing species. This large cat now lives from Alaska through Canada with small populations remaining mostly on federal lands in Montana and Washington State. Due mainly to trapping, hunting, logging, road building, and the construction and expansion of ski resorts, the lynx has been completely "eliminated from approximately seventeen states" in the New England, Great Lakes, Rocky Mountains, and Pacific Northwest regions. FWS scientists estimate that the number of lynx remaining in the lower forty-eight states "may not exceed several hundred, far fewer than many other species now listed as endangered." Today, the main threats to the remaining lynx include excessive logging in the national forests, and trapping, which is encouraged by the price that the cat's luxurious pelt can bring.

The FWS first placed the lynx under review for protection in the 1970s and even proposed to list it as "endangered" in 1982, but never did so. In 1994, the Biodiversity Legal Foundation petitioned FWS to place the lynx on the list. Agency biologists, supported by the scientific community, found the request to be warranted. Both the FWS Field Office in Helena, Montana, and the Rocky Mountain Regional Office in Denver, Colorado, approved the listing recommendation.

Then suddenly the listing was stopped in its tracks. PEER's White Paper describes what unfolded next: "The Washington, D.C., office of FWS then did something that was unprecedented. Acting Director Richard N. Smith overruled the regional listing recommendation, and ordered the Office to rewrite the finding as 'not warranted,' which was done." As PEER describes the decision, "The blatant disregard shown by the Director of FWS for the unanimous conclusion of FWS biologists in several regions can only be explained by a desire to satisfy the logging and development industries."

Soon, Defenders of Wildlife, The HSUS, and other wildlife protection groups filed a lawsuit to force FWS to list the lynx, and the D.C. District Court ruled in their favor. It found that the agency had ignored the "overwhelming consensus among its biologists . . . that the lynx must be listed." The federal court stated that the "glaringly faulty factual premises" used to avoid the listing were "contradicted by the entire administrative record."

On May 27, 1997, the FWS finally issued a finding that listing the lynx as endangered in the lower forty-eight states was "warranted." At the same time, it claimed that it could not actually take the time to list the lynx because of the need to work on other species that had higher priority. As PEER summarized the situation, "Suddenly FWS, which had had all the time and resources to fight listing the lynx for years, now could not make the small additional effort to finish the formal listing."[30]

Losing Other Vulnerable Species

Many other species of American wildlife have long been denied protection by the FWS because of political pressure from special interests.

The Alexander Archipelago wolf, for instance, is found only on a few islands in Alaska's heavily timbered Tongass National Forest. It is threatened mainly by trapping, hunting, and logging, especially the clear-cutting of old-growth forests. Although the local field office of the FWS has recommended that the wolf be listed as "threatened," the timber industry, the United States Forest Service, and the Alaskan Congressional delegation have successfully opposed this action.[31]

Fewer than 400 peninsular bighorn sheep now remain in mountain desert regions from southern California to Baja California, Mexico. Despite threats to the bighorns from domestic cattle, poachers, and developers, FWS has long refused to list and protect the species.[32]

The Barton Springs salamander is unique in that it spends its entire life in the water, and lives only in Barton Springs in Zilker Park, located in Austin, Texas. Urban development has so polluted and depleted the Barton Springs' water supply that by 1996, the population of its salamanders had been reduced to between three and seventy-three. This prompted responsible FWS biologists to give the salamander "top priority for listing as the most endangered among species deemed to face imminent, high magnitude threats" in the southwestern United States. But when the FWS proposed to list the salamander as endangered, real estate developers protested vigorously. As a result, Texas Governor George W. Bush wrote to the Department of the Interior expressing "deep concern" that the listing might limit the use of private property. As a result, the proposal was withdrawn.

After a local environmental group, Save Our Springs, sued to reverse the Interior's decision, District Court Judge Bunton concluded that the Interior Department's "decision was based on political considerations, rather than solely on scientific data as required by the law." Judge Bunton found that the Department had violated its legal duties "so egregiously" that he ordered it to list the salamander as endangered." Finally, on April 30, 1997, after years of delay, the salamander was listed as endangered.[33]

Other vulnerable species that continue to be denied protection include the river otter, the bobcat, and over 1,000 species of imperiled plants identified by Smithsonian Institution scientists in the 1970s. At that time, the plants were described as being in need of priority action. In some cases, they have already become extinct. Instead the FWS has spent an inordinate amount of time working on de-listing (removing) species that are already on the protected lists. These species include the California gray whale, three large species of Australian kangaroos, and some populations of the African leopard.

IMPERILING SPECIES AROUND THE WORLD

While the FWS has been ignoring the plight of domestic endangered wildlife, it has actively worked to obstruct and prevent the protection of other imperiled species around the world. This is true especially of those animals that are subject to exploitation by commercial or hunting interests.[34]

The Sinking Ark

Another recent White Paper by PEER entitled, "Noah's Ark Is Leaking," documents "the almost complete abandonment of international Endangered Species Act protections" by the FWS. The May 1997 report is actually written by unnamed scientific staffers of the FWS' Assistant Directorate for International Affairs (AIA), the very unit responsible for protecting foreign species of wildlife. It concludes that American policy is now "controlled by commercial interests."

The paper notes that the endangered lists of the United States "were once flagships for the worldwide effort to save that part of nature confronted with extinction. Today, U.S. protection of foreign species in jeopardy is a fragmentary relic, controlled by commercial interests. Years of studied inaction by USDI has left the vast majority of internationally recognized life in peril unprotected by U.S. law":

> The FWS Assistant Directorate for International Affairs
> (AIA) has converted endangered species operations into a

conduit for importation by commercial and sport hunting interests. Emphasis is now given to de-listings, reclassifications, special regulations, and permits that facilitate such importation . . . [35]

As the number of species facing extinction grows dramatically, FWS' process for trying to protect them has become increasingly moribund. The result, PEER's scientists point out, "is a de facto moratorium on foreign listings, a posture which flies in the face of the growing global endangered species crisis." During the past ten years, "during this explosive decline in world biodiversity, the U.S. Lists had a net gain . . . of about one percent of the internationally recognized growth in endangered mammal species."[36]

The reason the FWS has virtually halted the listing of foreign species is pressure from special interests that are harming or exploiting the species involved. As PEER's scientists point out, the lack of action "reflects the constant pressure on the bureaucracy from commercially and politically oriented constituencies. The FWS' AIA continues to concentrate its limited resources on the concerns of special interest groups seeking reduced protection of endangered species, while simultaneously ignoring the plight of the many foreign species that warrant increased protection and recognition." The result has been catastrophic for much of the world's wildlife.[37]

Killing and Selling Endangered Wildlife

Because of successful lobbying by hunting and commercial interest groups, and the responsiveness of the FWS to these groups, many imperiled species in foreign lands have continued to be hunted, traded and further endangered by Americans. Often the policy of allowing and even encouraging exploitation of imperiled wildlife is defended under the newly popular concept of "sustainable use." Discussed in detail in Chapter 7, this controversial practice is based on the belief that giving an animal economic value will encourage its conservation.

One of the best examples of how this concept can have disastrous results is the African elephant, which, after much prodding by conservation groups, was listed by the United States as "threatened" in 1978. But the FWS continued to allow the importation of hundreds of millions of dollars worth of elephant ivory into the country, as well as tusks and other hunting trophies. The international trade in these products continued unabated. As a result, in the following dozen years or so, two-thirds of the elephants in Africa were wiped out, mainly by ivory hunters and poachers.[38, 39, 40]

When the international trade in elephant ivory was finally banned by The Convention on International Trade in Endangered Species in Wild Flora and Fauna (CITES), poaching of elephants was immediately and drastically reduced, and the populations began to recover. However, under pressure from the United States, importing and exporting of elephant hunting trophies continued to be allowed. Recently, CITES has again acted to allow limited trade in ivory to resume. And despite repeated pleas from conservationists, FWS has refused to upgrade the elephant's status from "threatened" to "endangered," since this would force the agency to ban the import of sport-hunted trophies.[41, 42, 43]

In the case of several large and spectacular antelope species of the Middle East, it was pressure from hunters rather than commercial interests that obstructed efforts to protect the animals. In 1991, FWS' Office of Scientific Authority (OSA), the successor to the Office of Endangered Species that was abolished in 1987, proposed to classify the addax, dama gazelle, and scimitar-horned oryx as endangered. Even though there was no question of the endangered status of the magnificent North African antelope, owners of large ranches in Texas where imported animals were released for hunting expressed concern over placing the antelope on the list. They feared it might interfere with the ranches' activity and/or prevent the transporting of hunting trophies across state lines. As a result, the listing proposal has, in effect, been abandoned.[44]

Not even Australia's famous kangaroos are safe from the FWS' obsession with pro-exploitation. The agency has encouraged the killing of literally millions of these creatures for the American market. In so doing, the agency showed that it could act with determination when it wanted to.

In 1974, the three large species of kangaroo were listed as threatened. Imports of their products were banned because of the massive commercial killing of millions of these creatures each year for their hides (many of which ended up in the United States). The result? Better controls were placed on the exploitation of these kangaroos by the Australian states, and the threats to their survival were somewhat diminished. The ESA was actually working as intended!

However, due to pressure from hunting and commercial groups, and the government of Australia, the FWS decided to de-list the kangaroos during the final months of the Bush-Quayle Administration. The de-listing was finalized in March 1995. In describing the situation, PEER's government insiders stated that the FWS moved quickly and forcefully to complete the action, which left one to wonder "why such a relentless and expensive effort was made to complete the de-listing even to the point of rushing the draft proposal through various levels of the Interior Department in the last week before President Clinton was inaugurated in January 1993."[45]

Many other vulnerable and persecuted creatures remain victimized by the FWS. Asiatic black bears, for instance, are being killed off for their gall bladders and other body parts, which are used in traditional medicinal formulas, yet the species remains unlisted. This is also true of the Arabian wolf. The work required to list this animal was done years ago, but "the project was killed and all the work negated."[46]

Interestingly, while claiming that it lacks the resources to list many species, the FWS spends inordinate amounts of time de-listing species of interest to commercial traders. For example, in the early to mid 1990s, the Nile crocodile of Africa and the saltwater crocodile of Australia were downgraded from endangered to threatened. This was to permit the importing of their skins to be made into shoes, handbags, briefcases, belts, and other items.[47]

As PEER observes, these de-listing projects harm both the species involved and other creatures in dire need of protection, as well: "It is unclear why OSA is putting its limited funds for endangered species work into such efforts, while thousands of seriously jeopardized species around the world are in need of help. . . . Potential projects desperately in need of funding [are] being ignored by the U.S. at the same time strenuous effort is being made to officially facilitate importation of commercially valuable species."[48]

Indeed, FWS bias against listing species is so strong that it sometimes refuses to act even when creatures are on the verge of extinction and there are no outside objections to the listing. In 1980 and 1991, The International Council for Bird Preservation

(ICBP) petitioned the FWS to list a variety of endangered African birds. A proposal to list thirty of the birds was drafted by the FWS in April 1992. None of the birds was involved in commercial trade; listing them would not have affected anyone economically; and, when the proposal was finally published, there were no objections to it.[49]

Still, the FWS halted the listing process because they expressed concern that three or four of the birds might already be extinct! Once it was established that these birds did or might still exist, the thirty birds were finally listed on January 12, 1995—almost four years after receipt of ICBP's petition.[50]

AMERICA ABANDONS INTERNATIONAL LEADERSHIP

The *IUCN Red List of Threatened Animals* is probably the world's most authoritative compilation of creatures whose existence is in serious peril. It is published by the World Conservation Union, also known as the International Union for Conservation of Nature and Natural Resources (IUCN). In 1996, the book listed 4,361 species (but not subspecies) of mammals, birds, reptiles, amphibians, plants, and invertebrates not found in the United States.[51]

By contrast, the Interior Department's Fish and Wildlife Service's listing of foreign endangered and threatened species (including subspecies) contains just 580 listings, less than 13 percent of these found in the *Red List*. Among the species recognized by the IUCN but not the FWS are the Australian koala, the giant anteater, the hamadryas baboon, the red panda, the Andean flamingo, and literally thousands more species.[52]

When the updated *Red List* was released, it was greeted with exultation by Secretary of the Interior Bruce Babbitt, who described it as "probably the most thorough scientific assessment of the state of the world's wildlife ever undertaken. It clearly indicates that, unless people of all nations make extraordinary efforts, we face a looming catastrophe of almost Biblical proportions . . ."[53]

The *Red List*, however, contained almost eight times more listings than the Interior Department's list. FWS wildlife professionals eloquently explain in "Noah's Ark is Leaking" why it is important for America to at least recognize a species' endangerment, even if our ability to directly help may be limited:

Every single U.S. listing document contains a version of the following statement: "Recognition through listing encourages conservation measures by federal, international, and private agencies, groups, and individuals." The hard facts are that the great battles to save wildlife and wild places are being lost. The United States is the only nation that has the resources to prevent the "catastrophe" pointed out by Secretary Babbitt.[54]

Citing Secretary Babbitt's endorsement of the IUCN listings, PEER has petitioned FWS to add over 3,700 species to its protected lists. So far, however, meaningful action has not been forthcoming. This inaction could prove tragic to our vanishing wildlife. When the 1996 IUCN list was published, Babbitt called it "a clarion call to take action while we still can." He stated:

The IUCN's report shows that we must not only continue and accelerate these efforts here at home, but that we must extend them world-wide by offering our expertise and support in conservation activities. Our children and grandchildren should not be deprived of a world where these magnificent and diverse wild animals can still find places to exist and raise their young.[55]

A FUTURE FOR OUR CHILDREN?

For decades, we have known of and have been warned of the danger of depleting and destroying the world's species and biological systems. Now, we have reached the point at which we must act quickly and decisively to safeguard what remains. If not, we will soon pass a point of no return that will lead us to disaster.

This impending danger was well understood by author and naturalist Gerald Durrell, who called our abuse of the environment "a weird form of suicide, for we are bleeding our planet to death." In the foreword of the 1984 book, *Gaia: An Atlas of Planet Management*, Durrell wrote:

"We have set about the task of banishing ourselves from our own Garden of Eden—our planet earth. Perhaps banishment is the wrong word to use, for it assumes that there is somewhere else we can be banished to, and in our case, once we have ruined and used up this Eden, there is no other. . . . This beautiful and endangered planet is the only one we have."[56]

John Tuxill notes in his Worldwatch paper entitled "Losing Strands in the Web of Life," that no one is immune from dependence upon "the earth's endowment of natural communities. . . . The loss of species and populations and the resulting simplification of the natural world touches everyone, for no matter where or how we live, biodiversity underpins our existence . . ."[57]

But whether or not we can make the necessary changes and adjustments to safeguard our future remains to be seen. The history of human civilization is not encouraging. In his eloquent account of the largest animal ever to live on earth, one that was slaughtered into near extinction, Dr. George Small writes in his book *The Blue Whale:*

> The tragedy of the Blue Whale is in the reflection of an even greater one, that of man himself. What is the nature of a species that knowingly and without good reason exterminates another? When will man learn that he is but one form of life among countless thousands, each one of which is in some way related to and dependent on all the others? How long will man persist in the belief that he is the master of the earth rather than one of its guests?[58]

Harvard Professor Edward O. Wilson raised a similar question about our potential for self-destruction in his 1993 cover article in *The New York Times Magazine* entitled "Is Humanity Suicidal? We're Flirting with the Extinction of Our Species." He writes:

> Many of earth's vital resources are about to be exhausted . . . . Natural ecosystems . . . are being irreversibly degraded . . . we are dismantling a support system that is too complex to understand, let alone replace, in the foreseeable future . . . earth is destined to become an impoverished planet within a century if present trends continue.[59]

But, as John Tuxill observes, there is hope: "Humans, after all, are not dinosaurs. We can change":

> Even in the midst of the current mass extinction, we still largely control our destiny, but we are unwise to delay taking

action. The fate of untold numbers of species depends on it. And so does the fate of our children, in ways we can barely begin to conceive.[60]

Gerald Durrell would agree:

Most of nature—if it is not destroyed or corrupted by us— is a resource that is ever renewing itself. It offers us, if managed wisely, a never-ending largesse [But] at the present rate of progress, and unless something is done quickly, disaster stares us in the face.

"I wonder what the attitude will be," Durrell asks, "if in a hundred years time, this book is read by our starving grandchildren— and they see that this decimation of their inheritance was recognized, cures were available, and nothing was done?"[61]

7. SUSTAINABLE USE OR UNSUSTAINABLE SLAUGHTER?

In recent years, a storm of controversy has been raging in the conservation community. At the center of this storm is the question, "Should we be killing rare animals in order to save them?" Advocates of this bizarre strategy, so-called sustainable use, claim that wildlife, especially those species found in the developing nations of Africa, Asia, and Latin America, cannot survive unless they have some commercial value to humans.

Sustainable use is based upon the concept that wildlife, especially rare species, will not be tolerated or conserved and cannot survive in developing countries unless it has some kind of economic value. Thus, in order to give local people an incentive to conserve their wildlife, the animals must "pay their own way." In other words, wildlife must be used commercially—hunted and traded internationally—*provided the animals are killed or captured at a sustainable rate that does not wipe out the species.* Although this may sound sensible in theory, in practice, it doesn't work because commercial exploitation is inherently unsustainable.

Putting the theory of sustainable use into practice means, for instance, that the way to save elephants from extinction is to hunt them, trade in their ivory tusks, or sell elephant foot wastebaskets; the way to save parrots is to capture and sell them as pets; and the way to save crocodiles is to market their hides for shoes and handbags. These examples describe ways in which different wildlife species can "pay their own way." Of course, there are other humane ways—ecotourism and wildlife-watching trips, for instance—in which this can be done as well.

Killing animals to conserve them, however, is a bogus, long-discredited rationale to justify the cruel and destructive commercial exploitation of wildlife, a trade that has driven countless species to the brink of extinction, and continues to do so.

COMMERCIAL EXPLOITATION

Tens of millions of wild animals are killed every year for purely frivolous commercial purposes. Furbearing animals such as bobcats and raccoons are killed to make garments from their fur; kangaroos, lizards, and snakes are "harvested" for their skins, which are used in the manufacturing of gloves, shoes, belts, and purses; and birds, snakes, lizards, turtles, and fish are captured by the millions for the pet trade.

We see countless examples of the commercial exploitation of animals every day. Many marine creatures, especially whales, dolphins, and fish, are in peril. So many parrots have been trapped for the pet trade that many species are nearly extinct. But despite these troubling facts, the practice of sustainable use as the best means to conserve wildlife is gaining widespread acceptance, even among some conservation groups.

The truth is, it is simply not possible to use and trade in wildlife on such a huge scale without causing immense suffering and massive overkilling of the creatures involved. Wild animals are very rarely subjected to what are considered "humane" slaughter techniques. Bobcats and lynx caught in steel leghold traps can suffer for days before dying of starvation, dehydration, or from a blow or shot from the trapper. Kangaroos and reptiles are often bludgeoned to death or even skinned while they are still alive. Sharks are mutilated for their fins and then thrown back into the water. Creatures captured for the live-animal trade, such as parrots and monkeys, are treated grotesquely and often suffer shock and trauma; up to 80 percent of captured birds will die before reaching their final destination. The traditional way of capturing apes for the pet trade or medical labs is to shoot the mother and then seize the terrified infant.

History has demonstrated that sustainable use of wildlife is not possible when there is commercial value in the sale of the animal or its parts. Placing a price on an animal's head enhances the incentive for killing that creature. Commercial use actually helps drive the species towards extinction.

This is what the fight over sustainable use is all about, and what is at stake is no less than the survival of the world's remaining wildlife.

THE RALLYING CRY OF BIG GAME HUNTERS

The cause of wildlife conservation has traditionally involved protecting animals, forests, and other habitat. Much of the progress that has been made in protecting wildlife has consisted of passing and enforcing laws that ban the killing, capturing, and trading of vulnerable species, as well as establishing preserves where these animals and their habitat are safe from human disturbance.

But there is a new wind blowing through Africa and the conservation movement. Strategies once used to protect animals are now becoming outmoded, naive, and out-of-date. Many modern conservationists believe that in a natural world increasingly under siege, the best way to save animals—indeed the only viable way— is by giving them economic value, having them "pay their own way." This is done through international trade in live bodies or dead parts.[1]

This cruel exploitation of animals was once euphemistically called "consumptive wildlife management." Its new, even gentler and more scientific sounding term—sustainable use—has become the rallying cry of a new generation of big-game hunters and traffickers in wildlife. They have magically converted themselves, or at least their images, from destroyers of wildlife to its savior. Even government wildlife departments, international conservation agencies, and some powerful private conservation organizations have adopted the philosophy that imperiled species have to be killed in order to be saved. As the FWS' own biologists have written of its international endangered species program, "The prevailing philosophy governing [its] policies is 'conservation through utilization.'"[2]

In theory, the concept of sustainable use does have some appeal. As its advocates explain, wildlife populations, even threatened species, need to be "managed" so as to regulate the capture and/or killing of a certain number of the animals for commercial or sporting purposes. This provides economic incentives for poor nations to conserve these "renewable resources." This is especially true in the case of controversial and potentially dangerous creatures, such as leopards, crocodiles, and elephants—that can do harm and cause difficulties for people, livestock, and crops.

But as the theory goes, local people are more likely to tolerate wildlife, even predators, if they are bringing in revenue, such as from the sale of ivory tusks, horns, skins, fur, and hunting permits. Not only can these revenues be used to provide jobs, develop land, and improve the lives of villagers, they can also fund the acquisition of parks and wildlife habitats, and the hiring of rangers and antipoaching patrols.

Unfortunately, while this theory makes sense to westerners living in wealthy developed nations, in the real world it does not and cannot work as intended. Case after case in which sustainable use has been tried, it has created a commercial market for wildlife that has stimulated uncontrolled, unsustainable killing of the animals involved.

Like King Solomon's proposal to divide a baby claimed by two mothers, sustainable use has turned out to be provocative in theory but unworkable in application. Dividing up wildlife among various groups of "users" works no better than cutting babies in two. Indeed, an examination of the species and population groups of creatures that have been subjected to consumptive sustainable use shows that, almost without exception, these animals have been decimated, depleted, and destroyed. As a 1993 report by the United States Marine Mammal Commission observes, "Virtually all species and stocks of wild living resources . . . which are being harvested commercially, are being depleted. . . . Throughout most of the world, species and stocks of wildlife are declining, often rapidly." [3, 4]

THE NEAR EXTINCTION OF THE AFRICAN ELEPHANT

The ineffectiveness of the practice of sustainable use is seen through the classic example of the African elephant. It demonstrates the inability of the policy's proponents to recognize, until the eleventh hour, that the concept is not workable.

During the 1980s, when wildlife protectionists were trying to stem the massive slaughter of elephants by banning the ivory trade, governments and other conservation groups repeatedly assured us that the industry was not the culprit. Indeed, we were told that ivory trading, and especially sport hunting, was a beneficial form of sustainable use. They claimed it gave Africans and their governments economic incentives to prevent the depletion of these commercially valuable giants.

Unfortunately, things did not quite work out that way for the elephants. Between 1979 and 1989, its continental population was reduced by almost two-thirds, from between 1.2 and 1.5 million to perhaps 600,000—a loss of approximately 700,000 elephants within a decade.[5, 6] Despite international attempts to regulate the lucrative trade in elephant ivory, its price skyrocketed along with the number of animals being killed. Governments of developing countries did not have the resources to protect elephants from poachers, and by 1989, it was estimated that over 90 percent of the ivory trading in international commerce had been acquired illegally.[7]

This poaching orgy ceased only when the ivory trade was finally shut down in late 1989. In that year, the signatory nations of the Convention on International Trade in Endangered Species of Wild Fauna and Flora (CITES) agreed to ban trade in ivory by placing the African elephant on Appendix I, its "most endangered" category. Almost immediately, the poaching of elephants was drastically reduced, and populations throughout Africa began to recover.[8, 9]

The lesson here is clear: whereas trade or commercial use of elephants nearly caused them to be wiped out, a ban on the use or trade stopped most of the killing and saved the species, at least temporarily, from extinction.

The slaughter of most of Africa's elephants could have been avoided if the FWS and the international conservation community had not been so zealously committed to the philosophy of sustainable use. It had long been apparent that the large-scale killing of elephants was pushing the species towards extinction. In August 1977, The Fund for Animals formally petitioned FWS to list the African elephant as endangered, which would have banned the import of ivory. This would have removed much of the economic incentive for the then rampant poaching and focused international attention on the plight of the elephant, prompting other nations to take similar action.

However, a number of prestigious conservation organizations that support sustainable use, such as The World Wildlife Fund, the African Wildlife Foundation, and the World Conservation Union (or IUCN), actively opposed an ivory ban, as did the ivory industry and big game hunting groups, such as Safari Club International (SCI). Thus, in May 1978, the FWS responded to the Fund's petition by refusing to list the elephant as "endangered." Rather, it placed the animal in the less protective category of "threatened," which allowed most imports of ivory, as well as of hunting trophies, to continue. And continue it did, almost to the last elephant in Africa.[10, 11, 12]

The veteran FWS scientist who drafted the 1978 listing regulations, highly respected biologist Dr. Ronald Nowak, has since described the decision as "disastrous." He explained how harmful the agency's adherence to sustainable use has been for elephants. As he wrote in 1991:

> [The] constantly repeated argument that by giving the elephant (and other wildlife) an economic value, we will provide motivation and means for its conservation . . . has never been adequately supported. It was used in the development of the U.S. 1978 elephant regulations with disastrous results. [They] also emphasized the idea that the ivory trade was sustainable, socially acceptable, and of value as a conservation mechanism. This line of thinking contributed to the loss of nearly a million elephants in the period that has since passed. Let us learn from this historical experience and not repeat the same mistakes.[13]

Unfortunately, as we shall see, the United States government *has* continued to repeat its mistake of listening to the ivory and hunting lobby instead of conservationists.

Paying for Hunters to Shoot Elephants

By 1989, the United States government may not have seen the light regarding the African elephant, but it was feeling the heat. Public outrage over the well-publicized slaughter of elephants throughout Africa finally prompted the Bush-Quayle Administration to adopt a policy of supporting an international trade ban on ivory and to lobby for such a measure at that year's CITES meeting.

At the same time the FWS and the State Department were supporting the ivory ban, another branch of the government was working to oppose it. In that year, the United States Agency for International Development (USAID) began giving away millions of dollars to fund a project in the African nation of Zimbabwe that encouraged both the trophy hunting of elephants and the continuing trade in ivory.

In addition, taxpayers' money was provided to Zimbabwe's Communal Areas Management Program for Indigenous Resources (CAMPFIRE) to fund and promote trophy hunting of hippos, lions, zebras, giraffes, Cape buffalo, baboons, and even such imperiled species as leopards and elephants. Funding was also provided to groups in Zimbabwe such as Africa Resources Trust, which lobbies to make it easier to import ivory and trophies of endangered and threatened species into the United States.

By 1997, under Administrator J. Brian Atwood, USAID had given CAMPFIRE $7 million. It increased the foreign aid giveaway to $20 million over the next four years, even though HSUS vice president Wayne Pacelle pointed out that "the rural people who are supposed to be the primary beneficiaries of the program have no control over it or the profits. . . . Interestingly, a 1995 audit of USAID discovered that only five cents of every American dollar invested went to village households. Ironically, a live elephant can bring in a million dollars worth of tourist revenues in its lifetime." [14, 15]

Moreover, as a group of FWS scientific, law enforcement, and regulatory specialists explained in a 1966 report, "Tarnished Trophies," the revenues from trophy hunting do not necessarily filter down to the indigenous people for whom they were intended, and they may even be used to harm, not help, the local wildlife:

> The idea is that hunting actually benefits the species because the substantial hunting proceeds that go to the host government are supposed to fund conservation programs for the threatened game species. In reality, these safari revenues provide precious hard currency to poor Third World countries for general operations and, in some cases, fund development or livestock projects, which further jeopardize the game species.[16]

The HSUS, joined by other conservation groups such as The Fund for Animals and The Sierra Club, attempted to persuade Congress to kill the appropriation. This effort was led by Congressmen Jon Fox (R-PA), John Lewis (D-GA), Christopher Smith (R-NJ), and Maxine Waters (D-CA). But the funding was strongly supported by the Clinton-Gore Administration and such prohunting conservation groups as The National Wildlife Federation and the World Wildlife Fund. And although the Republican-controlled Congress had long boasted that it was rooting out waste, fraud, and abuse in the foreign aid program, the Fox amendment to cut the CAMPFIRE funds went down to defeat.[17]

Unfortunately, the issue of United States support for sport hunting of elephants had been settled years earlier. In 1989, The HSUS petitioned the FWS to upgrade the African elephant's status to "endangered." The agency responded by publishing a proposal on March 18, 1991, stating that "most populations of the African elephant . . . appeared endangered . . . the Service determined in the proposed rule that over-utilization of the African elephant for commercial purposes was of sufficient threat to warrant reclassification of most populations to endangered."[18]

But on August 10, 1992, the FWS reversed course, withdrawing its proposal to list the elephant as endangered. Apparently, this was done to continue the import of sport-hunted trophies and to keep the door open to future ivory imports from nations that practice sustainable use. As the FWS stated in its rulemaking:

> The Service supports both non-consumptive uses of African elephants as well as certain carefully regulated consumptive uses of African elephants as mechanisms for attaining revenues to enhance elephant and wildlife management throughout the African Continent.[19]

A year earlier in 1991, FWS biologist and elephant expert Ronald Nowak had anticipated the agency's action, and commented as a private citizen on the agency's proposed action:

> By keeping the elephant improperly classified unnecessarily, for the purpose of facilitating sport hunting, the Fish and Wildlife Service would be making a mockery of the Endangered Species Act. . . . By implying that the elephant is in less jeopardy in countries that participate in the international ivory trade . . . the U.S. is encouraging the commercial value of ivory and thus the destruction of elephant herds throughout Africa.[20]

Even more ominously, in recent years, CITES has allowed a renewal of limited trade in ivory from several African countries, raising fears that, with ivory once again perceived as a valuable commodity, the elephant massacres of the 1980s might resume once again.[21] In some areas, poaching is again on the rise.

Trophy Hunting in Africa

In Africa, shooting of elephants and other threatened and endangered species is big business. And so-called American "sportsmen" are among the major players.

In addition to elephants, the imperiled species most avidly sought include leopards, rhinos, cheetahs, and lechwes (a type of swamp antelope). Other species include rapidly disappearing zebras, lions, buffalo, and bushbucks. Indeed, in many areas of Africa, the large "game" animals are virtually being eliminated, primarily by hunters. And there is nothing new about hunters seeking out the rarest game. A "sportsman" using searchlights at night shot the last three cheetahs ever seen in India. The last Barbary lion in the wild was shot in Morocco in 1921.[22]

In 1993, filmmaker Dereck Joubert, who has produced award-winning documentaries for organizations such as National Geographic, called for a ban on hunting in Botswana, where he had lived, filmed, and observed the wildlife for over a dozen years. Blaming hunting for nearly destroying "one of the last wilderness areas in Africa," Joubert noted, "In 1983, when we first visited the area, we were astounded by the abundance of animals. . . . Records show that in the late 1970s, numbers of animals were at least 10 times what they are now."

Not only had Joubert regularly seen hunters overkilling wildlife, he reported that they acted illegally and unethically:

> With few exceptions, every hunter who has used this area has broken the law. Men shoot from the back of vehicles into buffalo herds, wounding animals and leaving them to die while they chase after the herd to shoot another. Lions and leopards are sometimes wounded, and when they run into thickets, a fire is set to flush them out.

At great personal risk to his career, Joubert continued to work in Botswana, and courageously called for "a national hunting ban

. . . the land can no longer sustain its impact. Hunting in its various forms has been the prime reason for making large portions of Botswana devoid of wildlife."[23, 24]

THE WILDLIFE KILLING LOBBY

Attempts by animal protectionists to save imperiled wildlife from hunters have often been frustrated by the power and influence of the trophy hunting lobby. The most active and effective of these groups is the 32,000 member Safari Club International (SCI), based in Tucson, Arizona. Its members include former President George Bush (honorary), former Vice President Dan Quayle, Montana Congressman Ron Marlenee, and thousands of wealthy sportsmen who donate approximately $13 million each year to the organization.[25]

SCI relentlessly lobbies and works to promote the hunting of rare species and to allow the import of such trophies into the United States. The group's attitude toward endangered wildlife became apparent in August 1978. At that time, SCI formally applied for permits to allow its members to shoot and import over 1,000 animals each year. These animals included various species listed by the Interior Department's Fish and Wildlife Service as "endangered" and were banned from import except by special permit.

Included on SCI's annual "wish list" of endangered creatures to be killed and imported were 5 gorillas, 5 orangutans, 10 snow leopards, 5 clouded leopards, 100 cheetahs, 25 tigers, 100 mountain zebras, 150 African leopards, and various crocodiles, impalas, deer, gazelles, and other endangered species.[26]

The permit application was eventually withdrawn due to strong opposition from wildlife protection groups. Unfortunately, SCI has been much more successful in pressuring the Department of the Interior to encourage the hunting and importation of trophies from several of the species at issue.

For example, the Department has removed from its endangered list some populations of the African leopard and the lechwe, downgrading their status to the less protective category of "threatened." SCI has also tried to have cheetahs downgraded and subject to trophy importation. And it has been very active in working to allow continued international trade in elephant tusks and trophies, and for their importation into the United States.

SCI persuaded Congress to amend the Marine Mammal Protection Act in 1994 to allow hunters to import polar bear trophies from Canada. This effort was led by Congressman Don Young of Alaska, who received $4,500 from SCI during the 1993–1994 congressional campaign. Congressman Young is chairman of the House Resources Committee, which has jurisdiction over wildlife protection laws such as the Marine Mammal Protection Act and the Endangered Species Act. During that 1993–1994 period, SCI donated $47,650 to members of Congress, mainly those belonging to the Congressional Sportsmen's Caucus, an avidly prohunting faction.[27, 28]

Interestingly, SCI may have an ulterior motive in trying to weaken the regulations under the ESA. As documented in the following pages, several of its most prominent members have been arrested and prosecuted for illegally hunting and/or importing protected species.[29, 30]

Government-Subsidized Trophy Hunting

Ironically, the United States government, and thus the American taxpayer, is helping to subsidize the hunting of endangered species, and saving big game hunters lots of money on their taxes.

Because of peculiarities in the way the tax code is enforced and interpreted by the Internal Revenue Service, hunters are actually encouraged to stalk the rarest of wildlife due to a tax deduction incentive on their safari expenses. Dr. Teresa M. Telecky, director of The HSUS Wildlife Trade Program, investigated this appalling incentive at length. Basically, this is how it works: A hunter travels abroad, kills one or more endangered species, and then donates or lends the "trophy" to a cooperative museum. He then deducts the cost of the trip plus the value of the trophy from his taxes, which can easily reach $35,000 to $50,000. Where large permit fees are involved, this cost can reach over $100,000.[31, 32]

In the 1980s, John Funderburg, former curator of the North Carolina Museum of Natural Sciences in Raleigh, worked with trophy hunters. Through these hunters, the museum received donations of over 1,800 "specimens "for scientific purposes," valued at some $8.4 million.[33] The "sportsmen," some of whom were named "associate curators" by Funderburg, not only received a tax break, but in some cases were also able to " borrow" back their trophies. For perpetrating this deception, Funderburg was charged with violating the federal Endangered Species Act (ESA). He was fined $5,000 and placed on probation.[34]

In 1997, millionaire trophy hunter Kenneth Behring traveled to Kazakhstan in central Asia and shot two highly endangered subspecies of argali sheep. Argali are the world's largest wild sheep, and the males are much sought-after by trophy hunters because of their magnificent sweeping rack of curled horns that can reach over six feet in length. Shortly after his trip, Behring made a $20 million donation to the Smithsonian Institution so that its National Museum of Natural History could establish the Kenneth E. Behring Family Hall of Mammals and display 200 of the animals he had shot.[35]

The Smithsonian then applied for permits from the FWS to import the endangered argali sheep, as well as trophies of four other rare sheep from Asia and a huge brown bear from Russia. On a subsequent SCI expedition to Mozambique, where it is illegal to hunt elephants, Behring's party shot three elephants (assertedly through a "special permit" to SCI). One of the elephants was described in the newsletter *Hunting Report* as "absolutely stupendous. . . . The largest of the tusks weighed a mind-boggling 92 pounds, and is thus one of the largest taken in Africa in recent years."[36]

The IRS has designated SCI a charitable and educational group; therefore, it is elegible for contributions from the public. SCI takes in some $13 million a year in tax-deductible donations. Members of SCI can even get a tax deduction by becoming "curators" of their trophies and declaring "part of their home as a wildlife museum." They can "donate" the trophies to SCI and then store and maintain the collection in their homes.[37]

A guide to the *Secrets of Tax Deductible Hunting* is available from SCI. It offers such money-saving schemes as "Keep the Monster," which advises the hunter to "donate everything collected on your hunt but the one animal you really need." There is also "Give Away the Monster," which advises to "donate your record book animal for the mouth-watering tax deduction. Use the tax savings to go on another hunt."[38]

Calling these techniques "a sort of frequent slayer program," writer Matthew Scully observes, "Hardly a wild creature on earth, however endangered or harmless, is spared from this onslaught in the name of conservation and charity. Maybe it's time for the IRS to set forth on a little safari of its own."[39]

These tax incentives have helped stimulate a surge in the number of big-game animals that are shot and imported into the United States. The numbers have increased from 27,205 in 1990 to 46,582 in 1993, many of which were listed as threatened or endangered.[40]

And what has been the attitude of the Department of the Interior to the startling increase in trophy imports of rare animals? A highlight of SCI's 1995 international conference was the auctioning of FWS permits to import argali trophies. FWS was even thoughtful enough to supply SCI with the permits in advance. The permits cost just $25, even though a safari to shoot an argali can cost a "sportsman" well over $50,000.[41, 42]

Sabotage From Within

The FWS' neglect of the wildlife under its jurisdiction may seem criminal. Sometimes, it literally is.

Indeed, it is easier to understand why the FWS has so freely issued permits for the importation of trophies of endangered species that have been shot by hunters, when one considers an amazing fact: Richard Mitchell was a key official in the FWS' endangered species program during the period of increasing trophy imports. A convicted felon, Mitchell was found guilty of illegally importing the same endangered species he was given the responsibility to protect.

The strange case of Richard Mitchell sheds much light on the power and influence that the hunting lobby exerts on its wholly owned subsidiary, the FWS. Mitchell was a scientist with the FWS' Assistant Directorate for International Affairs (AIA)—the agency responsible for foreign wildlife issues under the ESA and CITES. While on loan to the Smithsonian Institution for a year in 1988, Mitchell accompanied several American hunters on a trip to China, during which four endangered argali sheep were killed. He was their "big game hunting guide," as described by Congress' General Accounting Office (GAO), which investigated the matter.[43]

As part of the arrangement, years earlier in 1984, Mitchell had set up, with the help of Safari Club International, The American Ecological Union—a nonprofit organization that encouraged and organized hunting trips to China, ostensibly for the purpose of research and conservation. Mitchell was involved in three of the trips.[44]

Mitchell and his party ran afoul of the law during the trip on which they shot the argali sheep. Mitchell had declared that the argali trophies he was importing were not from an endangered or threatened subspecies. Three world experts, however, unanimously swore that the argali sheep were, so the trophies were seized by FWS inspectors in San Francisco.[45] However, one of the hunters, Clayton Williams, was a former Texas gubernatorial candidate. He and his wife, Modesta, had influential contacts within the Republican administration of President Ronald Reagan. Williams also obtained help from powerful members of Congress, including Senators Lloyd Bentsen (D-Texas) and Pete Wilson (R-California), and Representative Jack Fields (R-Texas).[46]

Eventually, the government dropped all charges against these "sportsmen" and actually returned their trophies to them. Even more amazingly, the Smithsonian paid over $650,000 of taxpayer money to Mitchell's private lawyer for defending him. In August 1991, the GAO reported this payment to be illegal.[47]

But none of this seemed to tarnish Mitchell's government career working on endangered species issues. He returned to the FWS as a staff biologist until he became embroiled in further legal troubles. In 1993, in another federal case, he was convicted of a felony—smuggling a urial sheep hide and other animal skins into the country. For this crime he received two years probation and a $1,000 fine.[48]

Even this conviction, did not cost Mitchell his job, and he remained at the FWS. He was assigned his former position with the Office of Scientific Authority (OSA) in the AIA, working on permit applications for endangered species imports. He was even given the job of compiling information on the urial sheep, so it could be downgraded in protection by CITES. Protests from international experts on these wild sheep were so vehement, however, the proposal was withdrawn.[49]

By 1994, Mitchell was serving as foreign endangered species liaison to OSA, with responsibilities for making recommendations on the listings of foreign endangered wildlife, including a proposal to re-list the argali sheep as endangered. He continued to serve in this position until June of 1996, some eight years after he was first caught trying to import the then-endangered argali sheep from China.[50]

A LONG HISTORY OF FAILURE

There is nothing new or surprising about the failure of sustainable use to save the African elephant and other exploited species from extinction. Indeed, sustainable use has actually helped bring it about. In the past, whenever animals have been subjected to such commercial exploitation, the outcome has been the same time and time again.

A recent thoroughly researched and documented book by John A. Hoyt, president emeritus of The HSUS, demolishes the myth that wild animals can ever be sustainably or humanely subjected to commercial trade. In *Animals in Peril: How "Sustainable Use" Is Wiping Out the World's Wildlife*, Hoyt cites case after case of species that are supposedly being "managed" on a sustainable basis, but which are being decimated instead.

Calling the "growing acceptance of this doctrine . . . one of the biggest dangers wildlife has ever faced," John Hoyt observes that, "Unlike other more obvious threats, such as the fur and ivory industries, sustainable use hides its commercially exploitative orientation under the guise of conservation. It speaks not of shooting, trapping, killing, or capturing animals, but rather of 'utilizing wildlife resources' for their own well-being."[51]

Before the concept of sustainable use became popular in the early 1990s, the guiding principle of wildlife management was known as maximum sustainable yield (MSY). Under it, the sustainable management of a number of animal species was supposedly assured. For instance, the public was told for decades that the eight species of great whales were being scientifically and sustainably managed with strict quotas based on hard data. By 1972, there were so few of these whales left, they had to be placed on the Interior Department's endangered list. Since then, only one of these species—the California gray whale—has staged a recovery. The rest still struggle to survive.

Most of these whales were not given protection until they were commercially extinct. Consider the blue whale, the largest creature ever to live on earth. Between 1900 and 1965, over 325,000 blue whales were reportedly taken. The season was finally closed when only a mere 20 blue whales could be found and killed in the Antarctic.[52]

Ironically, whales have proven to be worth more alive than dead. Tourists annually spend over $300 million on whale-watching trips—a good example of true sustainable use.[53]

Parrots are another heartbreaking example of creatures that have been subjected to commercial exploitation under the guise of a controlled and sustainable "harvest." Some 30 million birds are captured each year from the wild for the international pet trade. Up to 80 percent die before reaching their final destination. It is not surprising, therefore, that dozens of species of parrots, macaws, parakeets, cockatoos, and other birds are in danger of extinction.[54]

One humane and sustainable way in which parrots and other exotic birds can generate revenue for the poor in developing countries is through ecotourism. This is a relatively new concept of nature-oriented travel and tourism. Through ecotours, people travel to places for the specific purpose of viewing and photographing wildlife and other natural wonders. Viewing beautiful birds in their natural habitats in countries like Latin America has proven to be very beneficial for the local people and the birds as well. One observer has described the sight of "a kaleidoscope spectacle of hundreds of brilliantly colored but highly endangered macaws sitting nearly shoulder to shoulder along the water's edge."[55]

There are an almost endless number of other species and resources, now devastated, that were "sustainably managed" by the experts. These species include grizzly bears, California sardines, Peruvian anchovies, most stocks of exploited ocean fish, several species of seals and ducks, and ancient and tropical forests. At the same time they were being massively exploited, writes John Hoyt, "Many responsible scientists and wildlife officials spoke reassuringly about scientific resource management, sustainable utilization, strictly enforced quotas, extensive scientific data, and controls designed to assure the perpetuation of these 'renewable resources.'" The same pattern is being repeated today, he warns— "except that we are rapidly running out of creatures to subject to such 'sustainable' slaughter."[56]

WHY SUSTAINABLE USE CANNOT WORK

After decades of mismanagement and decimation of wildlife, a few perceptive and courageous scientists have had the courage to speak out against the currently fashionable fallacy that justifies old policies in new guises. One of the best exposés of sustainable use is, ironically, a 1993 government report by the United States Marine Mammal Commission. It directly addresses the limitations of scientists in trying to understand and manage complex ecosystems and organisms: "People's expectation of what science can do is greatly overrated. Many of those consulted also spoke of the arrogance of scientists, mostly fisheries biologists, as being a major obstacle to moving forward."[57]

This extensive government study, "Principles for Living Resource Conservation," authored by Dr. Lee M. Talbot, was also supported by the Fish and Wildlife Service, the National Marine Fisheries Service, and the Department of State. It minces no words in describing the sorry state of the world's managed wildlife. Warning that "Among those consulted, there is virtually unanimous concern for the future of living resources throughout the world," the report emphasizes that "virtually all species and stocks . . . being harvested commercially are being depleted." It also states, "The harvest itself is the principal cause of depletion. . . . Many have questioned whether it is possible to achieve sustainable management of most living resources.[58]

The Talbot report cites the tuna-dolphin situation in the eastern tropical Pacific, in which millions of dolphins have been drowned in the nets of tuna fishermen. Thousands continue to perish every year. A five-year, multi-million dollar research study under very favorable conditions "couldn't detect even a 40 percent change in the population," the study notes. Given the ignorance and unpredictability that govern most wildlife utilization situations, the report recommends that managers err on the side of caution, and that a "new principle of uncertainty" be adopted:

> An ecosystem is characterize by uncertainty . . . and therefore management must recognize uncertainty as an overriding factor . . . management decisions should include a safety factor to allow for the fact that knowledge is limited . . . . In practice, our knowledge is often seriously inadequate, and predictions are uncertain.[59]

Many of the same points are made in an article titled, "Uncertainty, Resource Exploitation, and Conservation: Lessons from History," which appeared in the April 2, 1993, issue of *Science*. Written by three respected scientists—Donald Ludwig, Ray Hilborn, and Carl Walters—the article talks of the "remarkable consistency in the history of resource exploitation: resources are inevitably over-exploited, often to the point of collapse or extinction," and they warn that we are making the same foolish and greedy mistakes that humans have been making for centuries.

The authors caution that despite numerous environmental disasters of the past, similar policies today that supposedly are based on sustainability, are doomed to failure:

> Such ideas reflect ignorance of the history of resource exploitation, and misunderstanding of the possibility of achieving scientific consensus concerning resources and the environment. . . . Initial overexploitation is not detectable until it is severe and often irreversible . . . [e]ven well-meaning attempts to exploit responsibly may lead to disastrous consequences.[60]

Ludwig, Hilborn, and Walters also assign to the scientific community much of the blame for past mistakes. They believe it "has helped to perpetuate the illusion of sustainable development through scientific and technological progress." They warn that "our lack of understanding and inability to predict, mandate a much more cautious approach to resource exploitation," and urge that people should "distrust claims of sustainability . . . past resource exploitation has seldom been sustainable."[61]

Even Valerius Geist, a respected mammalogist at the University of Calgary in Alberta, Canada, and advocate of hunting, criticizes the commercialization of wildlife, writing that "this approach to sustainability is invariably ineffective, with devastating consequences for conservation . . . a global luxury market in wildlife is compatible with neither conservation nor good economics."[62]

THE REAL WAY TO PROTECT WILDLIFE

We don't need fancy new names for the "kill 'em and sell 'em and save a few for next year" school of wildlife management as the organizing principle for saving endangered wildlife. The traditional tried-and-true principles and methods—essentially, protect a species and its habitat—have worked quite well when properly implemented.

As a group of FWS scientific, law enforcement, and regulatory specialists wrote in a 1996 report criticizing the way in which the FWS was enforcing the Endangered Species Act, "The 1972 U.S. listing of eight species of great whales and eight kinds of spotted and striped cats [tigers, cheetahs, leopards, jaguars, etc.] helped to cut off major markets for the products of those animals, and to inspire a worldwide movement that, up to now, has prevented their extinction." The international trade ban on elephant ivory enacted in 1989 by CITES at the urging of wildlife protectionists belatedly brought the massive poaching of elephants to a halt. Many other species have been saved from extinction by outlawing, not encouraging, their killing and the sale of their body parts.[63]

Ironically, much more money can be earned from viewing live animals over and over again than from killing them once. As John Hoyt points out in *Animals in Peril*, "There really is such a thing as true sustainable use . . . often involving carefully-controlled ecotourism activities such as the nondisruptive viewing of whales, parrots, gorillas, elephants, and other wildlife in their natural environments."[64]

Where humane sustainable use, such as ecotourism, falls short to many of its critics is in failing to provide elephant tusks to ivory merchants, animals skins to the fur industry, and parrots to the wild bird pet trade. It is controversial because it threatens the profits of certain industries and governments that benefit from the slaughter and suffering of wild animals.

Because humane sustainable use allows animals to live, it will always be opposed or belittled by those individuals and industries that rely on consumptive exploitation of wildlife, and by their allies in the conservation movement.

VALUING ANIMALS FOR THEIR OWN SAKE

What about those animals that are not of any particular interest to tourists, those that cannot " pay their own way"? These creatures also have a right to exist. As John Hoyt observes, "Until we decide to protect and preserve the natural environment and the creatures with which we share the earth—even those that do not appear to be immediately useful to us—our planet's future will be in peril, as will our own."[65]

John Hoyt is exactly right when he warns us that we may "one day awaken to find that our wildlife heritage has been stolen from us by those who know the price of every creature, but the value of none." The concept of "sustainable use of wildlife" is a bankrupt notion that capitalizes on brutality and death. What the natural world needs for the new millennium is not a philosophy of death, but rather a commitment to life—of humane stewardship—that glorifies and preserves the lives of all of God's creatures.[66]

It is only when we learn to appreciate animals for their own intrinsic value that there will there be hope for their salvation—and for ours. Their lives and their being must have value in and of themselves. This is the only true path of sustainability that will take us—all of us—into the new millennium with the hope of a secure future for our planet and our children.

PART IV

How We Can Save the Animals—And Ourselves

8. Towards a Humane Society

Mahatma Gandhi once said that "the greatness of a nation, and its moral progress, can be judged by the way that its animals are treated." Similarly, it is clear that if we can attain a truly humane society, it is not just animals that will benefit. Humans, as well, will be better off in numerous important ways, as they will live in communities that are cleaner and healthier; less violent and less polluted; and more peaceful, prosperous, and just.[1, 2]

LINKING ABUSE OF HUMANS AND ANIMALS

If there is one single collection of evidence that demonstrates beyond doubt how promoting kindness to animals can improve the lives of humans, it is this: The most brutal and senseless violence in our society, especially random murders by serial killers, usually begins with and progresses from abuse of animals. Thus, intervening to prevent violence towards animals can save human lives as well.

How Strong Is the Link?

The link between the abuse of animals and the abuse of people has been widely studied and extensively documented, and is well known among law enforcement officials, social workers, and animal welfare professionals. If society had intervened early in the lives of such mass murderers as Jeffrey Dahmer and David Berkowitz (Son of Sam), when these men were boys experimenting with cruelty to animals, the lives of many innocent people could have been saved.

The Humane Society of the United States (HSUS) has long been concerned about the link between cruelty to animals and abuse of humans, especially children and domestic partners. In 1986, Dr. Randall Lockwood and Guy Hodge wrote, "Stories of people who exhibit violence toward both human beings and animals are disturbingly common, and come as little surprise to those involved with animal welfare":

> The belief that one's treatment of animals is closely associated with the treatment of fellow human beings has a long history in philosophy. The idea served as the ethical foundation for the rise of the animal-welfare movement during the nineteenth century. . . . There is compelling circumstantial evidence linking two groups of criminals—serial and mass murderers—with acts of cruelty to animals. There is a significantly high incidence of such acts, usually prior to age twenty-five, among people who have engaged in multiple murders.
>
> Serial killers almost invariably have histories of animal abuse earlier in their lives . . . [and] the FBI has indicated that brutal and irrational serial killings account for one-quarter of all unsolved murders in the United States each year."[3]

Dr. Lockwood, a psychologist and an HSUS vice president, observes that his work over a twenty-year period "has demonstrated that animal abuse is present in nearly 90 percent of the pet-owning homes where there is physical abuse of children. Other colleagues have found that over 70 percent of pet-owning women who seek protection in women's shelters have had a loved pet threatened, injured, or killed by their abusers. The victimization of animals has also been associated with the abuse of the elderly and the disabled."[4]

Under the direction of Dr. Lockwood, The HSUS has a long history of working closely with local, state, and federal law-enforcement agencies on cases involving cruelty to animals. These officials have found that the investigation and prosecution of crimes against animals can be an important tool in identifying people who are already inflicting violence upon people, or who may do so in the future.

Special Agent Alan Brantley, of the Federal Bureau of Investigation's (FBI's) Behavioral Science Unit, is a psychologist who has interviewed and profiled many violent criminals, and is convinced that "you can look at cruelty to animals and cruelty to humans as a continuum":

> Our pets are friendly and affectionate, and they often symbolically represent the qualities and characteristics of human beings. Violence against them indicates violence that may well escalate into violence against humans. . . . People shouldn't discount animal abuse as a childish prank or childish experimentation.[5]

Consider the following studies:

❏ A 1985 study found that "a child who learns aggression against living creatures is more likely to rape, abuse, and kill other humans as an adult."[6]

❏ In a 1983 study, "in 88% of families . . . where physical abuse occurred, animals in that home were also abused. In about two-thirds of the cases, the abusive parent had killed or injured the animals to discipline the child."[7]

❏ A 1988 study of twenty-eight rapist-murderers found that 36 percent had engaged in acts of animal cruelty in childhood, and 46 percent during adolescence.[8]

❏ In a study of prison inmates, 48 percent of the rapists and 30 percent of the child molesters admitted to having been cruel to animals.[9]

How Mass Murderers Start Out

In real life, these statistics translate into tragedies for countless families, involving some of the most infamous mass murderers and serial killers:

❏ As a child, Jeffrey Dahmer enjoyed torturing animals, impaling frogs and cats, and beheading a dog. As an adult, he graduated to killing and dismembering at least seventeen people, freezing their body parts, and eating them.[10, 11]

❏ New York City's most notorious serial killer, David Berkowitz—called Son of Sam—was known by neighbors for killing local pets.[12, 13]

❏ Unabomber Ted Kaczynski, who killed and maimed people by mailing them letter bombs, had a history of abusing cats.[14, 15]

❏ Ted Bundy, who is thought to have killed over one hundred women in years of random murder sprees, enjoyed killing animals as a child.[16, 17]

❏ Albert DeSalvo, better known as the Boston Strangler, first learned to enjoy killing by trapping dogs and cats in orange crates and shooting them with arrows.[18, 19]

❏ Pedophile and child murderer Jesse Timmendequas endured years of childhood abuse, during which family pets were tortured in front of him. Later, his crimes against children inspired "Megan's Law," which requires that neighbors be notified of the presence of sex criminals.[20, 21]

❏ Outside Atlanta in 1998, Mark Barton shot his eight-year-old daughter's kitten, and then pretended to lead her on a search for the dead pet. A few months later, in July 1999, he went on a shooting rampage in Atlanta, killing thirteen people—including himself—and wounding thirteen others.[22]

A New Trend—Children Who Kill

In recent years, many youngsters have not waited until adulthood before committing mass murder:

❏ In April 1999, in Littleton, Colorado, Eric Harris, eighteen, and Dylan Klebold, seventeen, brought guns and bombs into Columbine High School. There, they killed a dozen of their fellow students and one teacher before killing themselves. These youngsters had often spoken of mutilating animals, and Klebold enjoyed shooting woodpeckers.[23]

❏ In Springfield, Oregon, in May 1998, Kip Kinkel, fifteen, walked into his high school cafeteria and opened fire, killing two classmates and wounding twenty-two others. His parents were found later that day, shot to death in their home. Kinkel had a long history of animal abuse and often bragged about torturing and killing animals.[24]

❏ In October 1997, in Pearl, Mississippi, Luke Woodham, sixteen, stabbed to death his mother and then went on to his school, where he shot and killed two students and wounded seven others. He had earlier written in his journal of the "true beauty" of beating, torturing, and killing his dog, Sparkle.[25]

❏ In May 1999, in Conyers, Georgia, Anthony "T.J." Solomon went on a shooting rampage at Heritage High School, injuring six students. His psychologist testified on his behalf that he was a troubled youth, and, "When he shot animals with guns, he loved to look into their eyes and watch them die and wonder what it was like on the other side."[26]

In numerous other cases of teen-agers killing other children, the murders were preceded by a well-documented history of violence towards animals.

Lessons to Be Learned

The lessons taught by the cases just cited are obvious, and were expressed as far back as 1693 by English philosopher John Locke (1632–1704), whose cogent insights on the origins of violence make him one of the earliest proponents of humane education. In his essay "Some Thoughts Concerning Education," Locke wrote, "People should be accustomed, from their cradles, to be tender to all sensible creatures, and to spoil or waste nothing at all."[27]

Anthropologist Margaret Mead explained that children get confused by the contradictory way in which we treat animals, killing some types for food while cherishing others as pets. She urged adults to explain this to children so that they don't get the mistaken notion that it's acceptable to kill pets. Mead wrote, "One of the most dangerous things that can happen to a child is to kill or torture an animal and get away with it."[28]

We must take care that the cruelty and killing we openly and unashamedly inflict on animals through trapping, hunting, and factory farming, do not teach our children the wrong lessons—lessons that will come back to haunt us in the form of school shootings, and child and spousal abuse. A society that condones large-scale, institutionalized, recreational killing of animals may be inadvertently encouraging susceptible individuals to commit acts of violence towards humans.

As Lockwood and Hodge point out, the best time to break the cycle of violence in our society is when a child first begins to resort to violence and abuse: "Within this tangled web, an abused child becomes violent to others, including animals. It is likely that he, too, is at risk of becoming an abusive parent who, in turn, may produce another generation of violent children."[29]

This was well understood by German philosopher Immanuel Kant (1724–1804), who observed, "He who is cruel to animals becomes hard also in his dealings with men. We can judge the heart of a man by his treatment of animals."[30]

EATING WITH CONSCIENCE

There are other important ways in which we can greatly enhance human welfare through improving the treatment of animals. One is "Eating With Conscience," an HSUS campaign I named and initiated that promotes a more humane diet. In *Eating With Conscience: The Bioethics of Food*, Dr. Michael Fox calls this "the most important consumer revolution of the . . . millennium—transforming how our food is grown and what we choose to eat."[31] Specifically, eating with conscience involves choosing foods that are good for your health, gentler on the planet, and kinder to the billions of animals raised for human consumption.

Good for Your Health

The standard American diet—high in meat, and low in fruits, vegetables, and grains—is widely considered unhealthy. As explained in Chapter 3, the drugs used by factory farm operations to speed the growth of food animals and prevent the spread of disease can be harmful to humans in many ways.[32] And, of course, a diet high in animal fat is known to contribute to the development of a number of degenerative disorders, including heart disease, cancer, stroke, diabetes, and obesity. While nonanimal products are less hazardous to health, many of the pesticides used on crops are known to cause cancer, miscarriages, and birth defects in animals, and are believed to be especially dangerous when consumed by infants and children.

On the other hand, a humane diet is now recognized not only as being kind to animals, but also as being healthy for humans. First, a humane diet limits or totally eliminates animal food. By being low in fat and cholesterol, it thus lowers the risk of many degenerative diseases. Second, a humane diet emphasizes the use of foods—both animal and nonanimal—that are raised organically and sustainably, and therefore are less likely to contain dangerous pesticides, drugs, and other potentially toxic chemicals.

Although no government group has specifically recommended a "humane diet" by name, the recommendations of the nation's major health organizations show that this type of diet is now widely viewed as being healthy. In 1996, even the strongly pro-agribusiness United States Department of Agriculture used its famous food guide pyramid to encourage the consumption of more fruit, vegetables, and grains, and less meat and other animal products. And in 1999, a number of organizations—including the American Heart Association, the American Cancer Society, the American Dietetic Association, the American Academy of Pediatrics, and the National Institutes of Health—approved a set of dietary guidelines that emphasize the consumption of fruit, vegetables, and cereal grains, and minimize the use of high-fat foods, especially animal products.[33]

Good for the Planet

As discussed in Chapter 3, the practices used to raise most farm animals and crops take a huge toll on natural resources, wildlife, and the environment. But much of this damage could be prevented or ameliorated if more farmers used humane and sustainable methods of farming.

Sustainable agriculture is environmentally sensitive. It uses farming methods that do not overwork the land or rob the soil of its fertility, and it ensures our ability to feed future generations. The techniques of sustainable agriculture include:

❑ Using rotational grazing techniques that shift livestock between pastures, and never exceed the land's carrying capacity.

❑ Practicing crop rotation and using cover crops to restore nutrients to the land and prevent soil erosion.

❑ Fertilizing fields with decayed organic material (compost) or manure from grazing animals.[34]

How to Adopt a Humane Diet

There is nothing radical or difficult about a humane diet. Indeed, it should be less expensive, more convenient, and better tasting than the average diet.

Many farmers, and especially those who work on family-run farms, use husbandry practices that are more humane and sustainable, allowing the animals to range free, socialize, graze, and live in a more or less natural manner. By promoting and buying products from such farmers, consumers can encourage demand for humane products, and decrease the number of animals that suffer on factory farms.

The key to following a humane diet is "the three R's":

❑ Reduce the amount of meat and other animal products you eat.

❑ Refine your diet by choosing foods that are grown organically, sustainably, and locally, and that come from farms which raise animals as humanely as possible.

❑ Replace animal-based foods with fruits, vegetables, and grains.

Wherever you might live, it is easy to find ways to choose a more humane diet. From major supermarket store chains to natural and health food stores, to food cooperatives and local farmers, many choices are available.

When it comes to dairy products, for example, try to avoid milk, yogurt, butter, cream, ice cream, and cheese that come from cows treated with recombinant growth hormone (BGH), a genetically engineered hormone designed to increase milk production. Instead, buy dairy products labeled "organic"—or, even better, try the many delicious alternative nondairy products, such as soy and rice milk.

Buy eggs that are labeled "organic" and that come from uncaged, free-roaming chickens. Or use a nonanimal substitute such as tofu.

Be sure to avoid the most inhumanely raised meats, such as milk-fed veal. This product is made from calves taken from their mothers at birth and forced to spend their lives in small crates, hardly able to move and fed heavy doses of chemicals, hormones, and antibiotics. Foie gras, often served as pâté, is made from the artificially fattened livers of geese force-fed through tubes stuck down their throats.[35]

Finally, keep in mind that there are many healthy and delicious meat substitutes, such as "veggie burgers," which are made from soy, grain, beans, and other vegetables. In October 1999, the United States Food and Drug Administration (FDA) stated that foods which contain soy protein can carry a label describing the food's role in reducing heart disease, so these foods are a good choice.[36] And you can make your overall diet more humane simply by replacing some meat dishes with your favorite meat substitute.

The Importance of Supporting Family Farms

Not too long ago, most of the world's food was produced by small farmers who supplied food for local communities. Now, as described in Chapter 3, small farmers are disappearing and being replaced by global corporations. These corporations turn out bumper crops with the help of pesticides, chemical fertilizers, and bioengineered, genetically mutated plants. Ironically, local people rarely benefit from increased food yields, since much of the harvest consists of luxury crops grown for export to foreign markets.

As the National Town Meeting for a Sustainable America points out, the key to promoting better agricultural practices—and of choosing a more humane diet—is purchasing food from local and regional farmers, especially those who use organic and sustainable methods:

> Our long-term food security depends on a consistent supply of healthy agricultural products from farmers who are sensitive to the quality of soils, water, and air. Consumers contribute to a sustainable food supply in their region when they purchase products from farmers whom they know are sensitive to the well-being of their environments and communities.
>
> It just makes sense that a community should be able to grow its own food. . . . Regional food systems, including food production, processing, and distribution, are vital components of a sustainable community.[37]

Yet today, such easy-to-produce goods as tomatoes, apples, and milk are commonly shipped across entire continents before they appear in our supermarkets. At a time when the average American or European meal travels 1,300 miles from field to plate, supporting local producers prevents much environmental havoc. It not only saves energy use and transportation packaging and costs, but also keeps money in the local economy.[38]

Local products are usually much fresher and more flavorful than those that are transported over long distances. The latter are often designed to have a lengthy "shelf life" and to withstand the rigors of shipping, storage, and refrigeration. Usually, this involves the use of chemicals that deplete the world's protective ozone layer.

The organic food industry is becoming increasingly important in supporting local farmers, contributing $4 billion in annual sales and growing by 20 percent each year since 1990. Consumers increasingly seek out food that has been grown "using methods that are in harmony with nature, healthy for people, and sensitive to the well-being of farm animals." Yet only about one percent of the United States food supply is produced organically, leaving much room for further growth of this industry in the years ahead.[39]

One popular way to support local farms and encourage humanely produced foods is to create community supported agriculture (CSA) groups. Such groups collect a fee at the start of the growing season, and then, on a weekly basis, provide fresh fruit for delivery to or pick up by customers. Another means of supporting local farms is the food cooperative (co-op), in which food is collected from a group of farmers and distributed monthly to members.[40]

Of course the most direct and satisfying way to eat more humanely is to grow your own food—in either your own garden or in a community plot. Not only does this give you control over your diet, but it also is a relaxing and enriching way to connect to the earth and to appreciate its miraculous ability to provide both vitamin- and mineral-rich food through the use of seeds, sunlight, soil, and water.

You can help promote family farmers by persuading your office cafeteria, high school and college officials, and food service managers to purchase food from local producers, especially those who use humane, organic, and sustainable methods of farming.

Suggest the same to the supermarkets and restaurants you patronize. If they do not respond, take your business elsewhere.

The best way to be an advocate for change is to vote with your wallet. As Michael Fox observes, "We can farm without harm, eat with conscience . . . regenerate our land, and recover our humanity."[41]

HOW SHOULD WE MEASURE OUR PROGRESS?

Using most economic indicators, America is the most advanced, prosperous, and successful society in history. Compared to any other society, anywhere at any time, we are doing very well. What, then, is the urgency to change things? The answer is simple: What we are doing is not sustainable.

The Gross Domestic Product

If many people are unaware of the importance of addressing the problems that undermine and threaten our future, it may be because our traditional ways of measuring progress do not take into account the suffering, waste, and depletion that result from inhumane and unsustainable economic and agricultural practices. Our nation uses the gross domestic product (GDP) to measure the country's economy. But the GDP assigns an arbitrary and inaccurate value—zero—to two of our nation's most precious resources, social cohesion and the natural environment. Thus, the cutting down of a forest and the ruining of a watershed may show up in the GDP as a positive transaction, while the preservation of a forest and its wildlife will not show up on the GDP at all.

As the San Francisco-based group Redefining Progress points out, it is those social and natural resources that national accounting fails to address which have "suffered such erosion in recent decades":

> The GDP makes no distinction between economic transactions that add well-being and those which diminish it; and it completely ignores the non-monetary contributions of families, communities, and the natural environment. As a result, the GDP masks the breakdown of the social structure and natural habitat; and worse, it portrays this breakdown as economic gain.[42]

The Genuine Progress Indicator

To address the distortions in national accounting, Redefining Progress has developed the Genuine Progress Indicator (GPI). The GPI was designed to provide a more accurate scorecard of our economic health by counting many positive contributions that the GDP ignores, and subtracting costs that are often considered beneficial.

Consider that the GDP—our current measure of the country's economy—measures as positive economic growth such environmental factors as borrowing and using up resources from future generations, and thereby "depleting the physical resource base available for tomorrow's" economy. It treats as "additions to well-being" many obviously negative factors, such as economic costs stemming from environmental and social instability and break-down. These can include legal fees, such as those generated by lawsuits; medical expenses, such as those incurred in the treatment of cancer and heart disease; and the repair of damaged property, such as that produced by crime and hurricanes. The GDP also adds in the repairing of past damage, often tallying pollution "as a double gain: once when it is created, and then again when it is cleaned up."

In contrast, the GPI *subtracts* from its indicators the depletion and degradation of such valuable resources as farmland, wetlands, forests, and rivers, as well as the costs of air and water pollution "as measured by actual damage to human health and the environment."[43] Similarly, the GPI treats as costs instead of gains such environmentally damaging activities as the burning of fossil fuels, including coal, oil, and gas; the use of nuclear energy; and the consumption of ozone-depleting chemicals such as CFCs.

Infinite Growth on a Finite Planet

Our country's misplaced economic priorities are far more apparent and damaging when applied internationally. The United States' vast material prosperity is the envy of most of the world, but attempts to help other nations match our growth have often proven counterproductive.

As author David Korten wrote in 1995, we are confusing means with ends, and should be focusing on sustainable livelihoods instead of economic growth:

Nearly fifty years of international development efforts . . . have achieved a sevenfold increase in global GNP [gross national product] since 1950. Yet, unemployment, poverty, and inequality continue to increase. The social fabric of family and community is disintegrating, and the ability of the ecosystem to support human life is being destroyed— all at accelerating rates. . . . Very simply, we have defined our goals in terms of growing economies to provide jobs— a means—rather than developing healthy sustainable human societies that provide people with secure and satis- fying livelihoods—an end.[44]

"Ultimately," Korten concludes, "many current public policies are self-defeating. A global economy that depends on consuming environmental resources faster than they can be regenerated destroys its own resource base."[45]

Indeed, the question that must be raised is this: How can we have infinite growth on a finite planet? Even if possible, efforts to raise the standards of living of people around the world to that of Americans, *in terms of per-capita consumption of resources*, would be environmentally devastating. Our ability to significantly expand the world economy in terms of traditional economics is quite lim- ited, since humans are already consuming so much of the earth's plant material—crops, trees, and forest products—that is produced worldwide.

As former World Bank senior economist Herman E. Daly wrote in 1992, calls for increasing the global economy by several fold are unrealistic: "If experts are correct in their calculations that the human economy currently uses one-fourth of the global net pri- mary product (NPP) of photosynthesis . . . [L]and-based ecosys- tems are the more relevant to humans, and we preempt 40 percent of the land-based NPP. . . " [46, 47]

Indeed, writer Edward Abbey has observed that unlimited growth for its own sake is the mentality of the cancer cell.

The Green National Product

Clifford Cobb and John B. Cobb suggest that what is needed is a "Green National Product." An index of sustainable economic wel- fare, the Green National Product "would tell us whether economic activity was making us better off or worse off," and would focus on "care for the earth and for all of the people who are sustained by it." According to Cobb and Cobb, "This new GNP would differ from the old GNP by addressing the long-term health of the planet and its inhabitants. In other words, sustainability would be a central issue in the new measure, rather than an afterthought."[48]

As Redefining Progress points out, there is an "urgent need to improve and broaden the accounting framework that steers public policy," for if we are to "preserve our social structure and natural habitat, we must develop means to estimate their contributions to our economic well-being." Truly, we must find a way to characterize the destruction of nature other than as a measurement of our increasing prosperity.[49]

CARING FOR THE EARTH

One of the first internationally accepted conservation projects seeking to reconcile human economic development with protection of the environment was a 1991 document, *Caring for the Earth: A Strategy for Sustainable Living. Caring for the Earth* was authored by three major conservation groups: the United Nations Environment Program (UNEP), the Worldwide Fund for Nature (WWF), and the World Conservation Union (IUCN).[50]

While the document in many ways supported the exploitation of wildlife, it did contain some revolutionary new principles that endorsed the intrinsic value of animals and nature. It begins by warning that in heedlessly disregarding environmental concerns and living unsustainably, humans are "gambling with survival":

> Our civilizations are at risk because we are misusing natural resources and disturbing natural systems. We are pressing the Earth to the limits of its capacity. . . . The capacity of the Earth to support human and other life has been significantly diminished.[51]

The document stresses the importance of protecting the biosphere in all of its myriad parts:

> Biological diversity should be conserved as a matter of principle, because all species deserve respect regardless of their use to humanity, and because they are all components of our life support system. Biological diversity also pro-

vides us with economic benefits, and adds greatly to the quality of our lives. . . .

The diversity of nature is a source of beauty, enjoyment, understanding, and knowledge—a foundation for human creativity and a subject for study. It is the source of all biological wealth—supplying all of our food, much of our raw materials. . . .[52]

What is unprecedented for a document of this type is its endorsement of humane considerations and recognition of the innate integrity of other creatures:

Every life form warrants respect independently of its worth to people. Human development should not threaten the integrity of nature or the survival of other species. People should treat all creatures decently, and protect them from cruelty, avoidable suffering, and unnecessary killing.[53]

FREE TRADE VS. THE ENVIRONMENT

Unfortunately, instead of reorienting our international economic policies towards protecting the environment, small farmers, and local communities, the decade of the 1990s saw just the opposite take place. International trade agreements, such as the General Agreement on Tariffs and Trade (GATT) and the North American Free Trade Agreement (NAFTA), have not only undermined conservation efforts worldwide, but have also prevented individual nations from exercising their own sovereignty and enforcing their national environmental protection laws, especially those restricting imports of protected species.

And all this has taken place under the banner of "globalization," a euphemism under which multinational corporations evade the national laws that regulate potentially harmful activities by setting basic environmental, health, and food safety standards.

In 1994, the World Trade Organization (WTO) was created to promote and enforce "free trade." This secretive, unelected bureaucracy, based in Geneva, has the power to determine whether any law protecting endangered wildlife, ancient forests, public health, food safety, clean air and water, human rights, culture, labor standards (especially child labor), or anything else constitutes an illegal "barrier to trade" by WTO standards. If so, the body can demand that the law be abolished or that harsh sanctions be imposed on the offending nation. Cases are decided in secret by tribunals of three judges—usually labor lawyers—in closed chambers. Often, no explanations are given for the rulings made.[54, 55, 56, 57, 58, 59]

Already, the WTO has ruled against the United States' Clean Air Act, decreeing that its automobile fuel standards were unfair to oil companies that produce dirty oil. As a result, the Clinton-Gore Administration weakened the gasoline regulations to allow cars to emit dirtier exhaust, thus dooming thousands of Americans to increased illness, and some to death.[60, 61, 62, 63]

Under GATT—which is now part of the WTO—provisions of the Marine Mammal Protection Act limiting the killing of dolphins by tuna fishermen were deemed illegal, as were Endangered Species Act regulations protecting imperiled sea turtles. Also overturned were European Union laws banning steel-jaw leg-hold traps and the testing of cosmetics on animals when alternatives are available; a United Nations global moratorium on high seas drift-net fishing; and a Canadian plan to restrict imports of puppies from American puppy mills. For wildlife, the WTO is the single most destructive international organization ever formed.[64, 65, 66]

Other countries that tried to protect their citizens' health have been similarly stymied by the WTO. The WTO has ruled that the European Union could not ban imports of beef containing suspected cancer-causing hormones, and that Japan could not prohibit the import of fruit infested with exotic pests. Under NAFTA, Canada was forced to cancel its ban on the gasoline additive MMT, which can cause nerve damage.[67] And the WTO supported the Clinton-Gore Administration's challenge to Europe to stop giving preference to bananas grown by small, independent growers in the Caribbean. Instead, it ruled in favor of the giant corporation Chiquita Bananas, which grows its fruit plantation-style.[68, 69]

With the WTO encouraging virtually unrestricted free trade, the wildlife and environmental protection laws in its 135 member nations around the globe are potentially in jeopardy. Also threatened are the many American jobs now being given to people in nations with lower wages and weaker labor and environmental laws. The massive demonstrations in Seattle at the November 1999 WTO meeting showed the public's distaste for the organization's destructive actions.

THE EARTH CHARTER

Although individuals and organizations around the globe have taken steps to avert the destruction of the world's ecosystems, it is clear that the tides of destruction have continued to rise. It was an awareness of this rising tide that led to the creation of the Earth Charter—a charter that seeks to redefine our relationship with the planet on which we live.

Planting the Seeds for the Charter

The seeds for the Earth Charter were planted in 1987, when the United Nations World Commission on Environment and Development called for a document to be drafted to "prescribe new norms for state and interstate behavior needed to maintain livelihoods and life on our shared planet." As Steven C. Rockefeller, Chair of the Earth Charter Drafting Committee, observes, what is needed is "an integrated vision of the basic ethical principles and practical guidelines that should govern the conduct of people and nations in their relations with each other and the earth. . . ." The declaration would therefore draw on "the discoveries of science, the moral insights of the world's religions, and the extensive world literature on global ethics . . . and emphasize values and principles that are of enduring significance and that reflect the shared values of people of all races, cultures, and religions."[70]

By 1992, when the Earth Summit in Rio de Janeiro was convened, a growing number of people had begun to realize the need to work together to create such an ethical framework. One of the leading international figures of the twentieth century, Maurice Strong, was a prime organizer and the visionary secretary general of the summit. As he had said in 1987, "A firm commitment on the part of all nations and peoples to a new integrated ethical vision is essential if humanity is to achieve the goal of sustainability and insure the well-being of people and the larger community of life on earth."[71]

The Purpose of the Charter

After years of meetings and discussions with people and organizations from across the globe, the key document that exemplifies this ethical vision—the Earth Charter—was largely agreed upon. A statement of principles and ideas, the Earth Charter attempts to define the relationship of humans with the planet.[72]

The purpose of the Earth Charter is similar to that of the 1948 United Nations Declaration of Human Rights, which, although not a binding legal document, has been instrumental in creating a commonly accepted standard by which the nations of the world could be judged and pressured to conform to. The declaration has stimulated much progress in the field of human rights, including several important treaties and international agreements.

The supporters of the Earth Charter believe that it "has the potential to play a comparable role in transforming humanity's relationship with the natural world and the community of life." They observe that "the Earth Charter has an ethical framework that can be incorporated into future agreements and treaties, used as a standard to judge the behavior of nations, and employed by [citizens' groups] around the world to press for needed reforms."[73]

Key Concepts of the Charter

The Earth Charter, a collection of ethical principles for living in harmony with the earth and other creatures, presents a new way of thinking about the human relationship with nature. Some of its key concepts are the following:

1. All Life Has Intrinsic Value.

    The concept that the Earth and all life have intrinsic worth and deserve consideration independent of their usefulness to humans moves beyond the traditional economic view of non-human species as "natural resources," and gives more weight to non-quantifiable values such as biodiversity.

2. We Have Obligations to Future Generations.

    Acceptance of the principle that the current generation has obligations to future ones to pass on intact, rather than destroying, the natural environment, will help secure Earth's abundance and beauty for those who follow us.

3. Pay Heed to the Precautionary Principle.

    Adoption of the principle that, where there is a risk of irreversible harm to the environment, lack of complete certainty and conclusive data should not be used as a rationale to postpone necessary action.

4. A Global Partnership for Sustainable Development.

The goal of sustainable development is full human development while protecting the environment, and recognizing that our social, economic, environmental, ethical, cultural, and spiritual problems and aspirations are all interconnected.[74]

Objectives of the Earth Charter Campaign

In 1997, an Earth Charter Commission, based at the Earth Council in Costa Rica, was established to supervise the drafting of the charter. Thirty-five national committees from all regions of the world were formed to organize a worldwide dialogue on shared values and ethics. This dialogue would involve all religious, cultural, ethnic, and national groups. In April 1999, the Center for Respect of Life and Environment (CRLE) launched a drive, called The Earth Charter USA Campaign, to mobilize support for the charter. One of the project's goals is to have the United Nations endorse the charter, and have its principles incorporated into both the codes of conduct and the formal rules of government agencies and organizations in numerous sectors of society.

The Earth Charter USA National Committee, headed by John A. Hoyt, is composed of leaders from key sectors of American society, including grassroots and citizens groups, religious organizations from all faiths, labor and business groups, and representatives from government, politics, and the academic community.

The Choice Is Ours

The Preamble of the Earth Charter eloquently sets forth the choice facing humanity: "Fundamental changes in our attitudes, values, and ways of living are necessary. The choice is ours: to care for the Earth and one another, or to participate in the destruction of ourselves and the diversity of life":

In our diverse yet increasingly interdependent world, it is imperative that we, the people of Earth, declare our responsibility to one another, to the greater community of life, and to future generations. We are one human family and one Earth community with a common destiny.

Humanity is part of a vast evolving universe. Earth, our home, is alive with a unique community of life. The well-being of people and the biosphere depends upon preserving clean air, pure waters, fertile soils, and a rich variety of plants, animals, and ecosystems. The global environment with its finite resources is a primary common concern of all humanity. The protection of Earth's vitality, diversity, and beauty is a sacred trust.[75]

The charter says that seeking renewal and a new beginning will require "an inner change—a change of mind and heart," requiring that we take "decisive action to adopt, apply, and develop the vision of the Earth Charter. Every individual, family, organization, and government has a critical role to play":

> We must recognize that human development is not just about having more, but also about being more. The challenges humanity faces can only be met if people everywhere acquire an awareness of global interdependence, identify themselves with the larger world, and decide to live with a sense of universal responsibility.[76]

In order to accomplish this, we must strengthen "the spirit of human solidarity and kinship with all life," and begin to "live with reverence for the sources of our being, gratitude for the gift of life, and humility regarding the human place in the larger scheme of things."[77]

THE POWER OF EARTH DAY

There are many ways in which groups and individuals can spread awareness of the plight of the planet. One means is the annual Earth Day celebrations held across the globe.

The Goal of Earth Day

Jan Hartke, a close ally of Earth Day founder Denis Hayes, has been a leader in the effort to create and establish the event as a permanent worldwide tradition. Hartke believes that Earth Day can "power the environmental movement through the new millennium," and have "an ongoing impact throughout the year":

> We can mobilize hundreds of millions of people, transforming local, national, and international institutions. Earth Day, and what it stands for, is accessible to all, a potential

well-spring of inspiration for the young people who will inevitably be given the keys of stewardship for the earth and all its creatures.[78]

According to Hartke, the essence of Earth Day is "a fundamental redefinition of the human/earth relationship, fostering a humane, just, mutually enhancing, and ecological worldview":

> We share a physical, evolutionary, and spiritual kinship with all creation. This reality gives us the innate capacity to empathize with all of the earth's life forms, to touch the deepest chords of our being, and feel a part of the vast, subtle, mysterious connections and interdependence that we have with all creation.
>
> Empathy, the capacity to see through the eyes of other creatures, changes everything. Empathy has a certain magical quality, it is the precondition to caring. Seeing through the eyes of another creature or being evokes a sense of compassion, justice, respect, reverence, and love. In this deeply profound way, Earth Day can change the world.
>
> Interior Secretary Bruce Babbitt has observed that a "grand convergence" is emerging between the humane and environmental movements. I agree. It is in that spirit that I joined the International Council of the Earth Day Network and supported the Earth Day events for the last decade. As we enter the new millennium, we expect . . . to mobilize 500 million people around the globe to celebrate the earth and the diversity of life on the planet. While Earth Day is only one of the countless examples of outreach and activism, it is an outstanding model because its reach is global, ongoing, and personal.[79]

In keeping with a wide array of educational outreach efforts, such as The HSUS's KIND News for school children, the mobilization effort of Earth Day can awaken people to their moral responsibility to be good stewards of our natural heritage and our moral responsibilities to animals. Just as Earth Day 1990 helped lay the foundation for the historic Earth Day Summit of 1992, so, too, can the outreach and activism associated with each Earth Day in the new millennium move our world closer to a clean, safe, efficient, and renewable energy system; provide greater impetus to the national effort to encourage the government to protect 60 million acres of pristine habitat in our national forests; and deepen the demand of citizens everywhere for a humane, just, and sustainable earth ethic.

The Earth Day tradition also serves to illustrate the utmost importance of working with partners and allies who share our humane and environmental perspectives. Organizing the vast network of concerned citizens to get involved and engaged in the great work of our times—the noble endeavor to save and protect the beauty, diversity, and life of the planet—is extraordinarily important. Only by working with others and finding common ground can we shape the kind of world we want. It is hoped that, in the years and decades and centuries to come, the humane and ecological values espoused by Earth Day will make it one of the most widely celebrated, uniquely global traditions in human history.

Making Every Day, Earth Day

Making "Earth Day, Every Day" is a mission worthy of our best efforts and a lifetime of dedication. A major step towards realizing this goal was taken when three key players came together to eliminate the overlap and confusion in observing global environmental events.

At a meeting between Earth Day Network Chairman Denis Hayes; Klaus Toepfer, administrator of the United Nations Environment Program (UNEP); and Energy Secretary Bill Richardson, it was agreed that Earth Day would be recognized globally on April 22 of each year, and United Nations World Environment Day would be celebrated on June 5 of each year. Between these dates, there would be a campaign season for the earth.[80] Thus, while the first Earth Day emerged in 1970 as an American experience, its activities and those associated with World Environment Day are now celebrated throughout the world.

Earth Day has come a long way since its inception in 1970. It has become a testimony to people's love for the earth and its creatures. It inspires the turnout of huge numbers of people around the world. It is headlined by celebrities of all types. And it grabs the attention of political leaders, corporations, business interests, and news media throughout the globe.

Yet when the long term is considered, it seems clear that Earth Day will also become an intimate personal and family time as well.

The shift in consciousness and behavior that we seek needs to take place in our hearts, to be practiced in our lives, and to be conveyed to our children in thought as well as deed. Ultimately, society changes gradually, one person at a time, one action at a time. We will end up saving only what we, as individuals and families, really care about. At this millennial crossroads, the fate of the animals, and of the earth, is truly in our hands.

ARE WE MAKING PROGRESS?

If we can put in place the principles and actions discussed above, we can truly attain a humane and sustainable society. We know what to do, and we know how to do it. The question thus is not *can* we, but *will* we?

One Step at a Time

Albert Schweitzer understood that humanity would not find tranquility until this was granted to other life forms, warning that "without a reverence for all life, we will never have world peace." But he was not optimistic about humanity's ability to act with restraint, saying that "mankind has lost the capacity to foresee and to forestall; he will end by destroying the earth."[81, 82]

Still, Schweitzer understood how long it can take for people to adopt new ways of thinking about moral and ethical matters. He knew that progress comes slowly. In 1923, in *Civilization and Ethics*, he predicted that "the time is coming . . . when people will be astonished that mankind needed so long a time to learn to regard thoughtless injury to life as incompatible with ethics."[83]

Similarly, the Reverend Andrew Linzey writes that theology "is still in its infancy. . . . It took the churches 1,800 years to recognize that you can't love God and keep humans as slaves. . . . What we now have to learn is that we cannot love God and hate his non-human creatures." Linzey maintains that our best hope of improving human treatment of animals is gradual progress, "progressive disengagement from our inhumanity to animals":

> The urgent and essential task is to invite, encourage, support and welcome those who want to take some steps along the road to a more peaceful world with the non-human creation. . . . What is important is that we all move some way on if only by one step at a time, however falteringly. . . .

If we can persuade an intensive farmer to refrain from
de-beaking one hen, then at least some small burden of suffering is lessened in the world.[84]

Linzey asserts, in effect, that in seeking change in our society,
the self-imposed requirement that we do only "the best" can be the
enemy of the good:

The enemy of progress is the view that everything must
be changed before some real gains can be secured. . . .
But what is essential for this new world to emerge is the
sense that each of us can change our individual worlds,
however slightly, to live more peaceably with our nonhuman neighbors.[85]

Contradictions abound in our society. Some animals—pet dogs
and cats, for instance—are generally treated with love, while similar creatures—coyotes and bobcats—are eagerly killed for "sport."
This anomaly has been referred to as "Rowan's Paradox," after
HSUS Senior Vice President Andrew Rowan. He noted the irony in
legally regulating the treatment of laboratory mice in cages, while
in the same building, escaped or wild mice are trapped on excruci-
atingly painful glue boards. In large parts of India, cows are
revered and not killed, but are allowed to suffer dreadfully in the
streets.[86]

Over Three Hundred Years of Humane Action

Despite the contradictions noted by Andrew Rowan, we are clearly making progress by forming the moral basis for a more humane
society. It has been well over three hundred years since America
gained the distinction of being the first western nation to pass a
law banning cruel treatment of animals. In 1641, the Puritans who
founded the Massachusetts Bay Colony enacted a legal code that
included Liberty 92: "Cruelty to animals forbidden." It was almost
another two hundred years before another state, New York, passed
an anticruelty statute.[87]

It was not until after the American Civil War (1861–1865) that
the humane movement began to attract widespread support. In
1865, Henry Bergh traveled to London and visited the Royal Society for the Protection of Animals, then in its forty-first year. He
decided to form a similar organization in America. The following

year, the American Society for the Prevention of Cruelty to Animals (ASPCA) was chartered in New York City, and Bergh was named president of what was the first real humane society in the Western Hemisphere. In the years to follow, other humane societies were established throughout the United States to care for injured, abused, and stray animals.[88, 89]

It is interesting to note that for centuries, the term "humane" was used to designate only those groups dedicated to helping *humans* in distress.[90] In the late 1700s, the term began to appear in the names of organizations devoted to rescuing victims of drowning and shipwrecks, starting with the formation of a Dutch society in Amsterdam in 1767, and a British one in 1774. Similar humane societies sprang up in the northeastern United States, and such groups gradually expanded their efforts to help debtors, children, the sick, and the indigent. By the early 1800s, numerous humane societies were working on the abolition of slavery. It was not until 1869 that "humane" was used in the title of an animal protection group, when the Illinois Humane Society was founded.[91]

In modern times, the state has taken over most of the responsibilities for helping people in distress, leaving only animal abuse to be handled largely by the private sector. "Humane" has now come to refer to the care of nonhuman creatures, but the broader use of the term better expresses the all-encompassing compassion that would characterize a truly humane society.

Humanitarian Bernard Unte has extensively researched the history and significance of the link between helping animals and human progress, pointing out that "during the past several centuries, a number of thinkers have asserted that the relationship between humans and animals has special import for the notion of a humane society." Indeed, he notes, "Animals present a special test of our broad commitment to a better society, for they are, ultimately, dependent on us."[92]

Unte goes on to observe that the humane initiatives of the last three centuries "shared the common denominator of concern for the elimination of suffering. . . . One of the most enduring elements of humanness as a concept is heightened concern for the elimination of pain":

> In past centuries, humans have better appreciated the mutually reinforcing qualities of concern for the relief of

suffering and exploitation in a wide range of areas. The movement for improved treatment of animals was lauded by many as a significant step forward in human social evolution. Indeed, it was frequently celebrated as a sign of a given society's claim to humaneness.[93]

A Single Community

In his 1992 book *Earth in the Balance*, Vice President Al Gore wrote, "We must make the rescue of the environment the central organizing principle for civilization." But in a truly humane society, we must also rescue our fellow creatures from the massive, pervasive, unending abuse to which they are being constantly subjected. And this will require, on our part, giving them the consideration to which they are entitled.[94]

Jan Hartke sees the concerns for the environment and for animals someday coming together. This pending fusion of movements is reflected in the words of Bruce Babbitt, whom Hartke, along with Stewart Udall, calls "one of the best secretaries of Interior in American history . . . [with] a unique sensitivity to the inextricable bond between the ecological movement and the values of a humane society."[95] Babbitt himself pointed out:

> Ultimately, there isn't a chance of persuading people, civilizations, and countries to take biodiversity seriously unless they first understand, from the depths of the human spirit, the need to relate to Creation, to be sensitive to the realities of suffering and mistreatment, and to have a larger, holistic, spiritual view of what Creation is about."[96]

The best way to move forward, according to Babbitt, is with "a deep understanding that a society that can allow animals to innocently get caught in a steel trap and die an agonizing death under the sun can't possibly have the spiritual strength to deal with all of the issues of habitat, biodiversity, and living thoughtfully on the land":

> The environmental movement has been a good while coming to understand that. I think we now understand that the human spirit has to accept the responsibilities that we, as one species, have at the apex of Creation, to make space for the rest of Creation to play its assigned role on this planet,

and to do it in a thoughtful and compassionate and reasonable way.[97, 98]

Richard M. Clugston, Director of the Center for Respect of Life and Environment, sees hopeful signs that "our culture is slowly awakening from the arrogance and autism of the materialist . . . world view." In the center's publication, *Earth Ethics*, he writes, "We are beginning to abandon assumptions common to the modern era that animals and natural systems are merely assemblages of inert matter, devoid of sentience, to be used by us as we wish." He believes that we can eliminate the inhumane behavior that persists in our society by adopting "a coherent and compelling earth ethic." This ethic would emphasize our responsibilities to preserve the integrity, beauty, and stability of biotic communities; to respect and enhance the well-being of each individual life, human and nonhuman; and to recognize our intimate spiritual interconnectedness with all life.[99]

Educator Marilyn Wilhelm, founder of the Wilhelm Schole International School in Houston, has an even broader outlook, calling the cosmos "a kinship system. . . . All nature is one unity, and the all pervasive universal principle of unity is Love. . . . Survival requires an active spiritual kinship with our fellow human beings and the world."[100]

Thomas Berry writes that "the renewal of life on the planet must be based on establishing the continuity between the human and the non-human as a single integral community."[101] Michael Fox writes of the circle we should draw—"a boundless circle of compassion to include all creatures and Creation within the scope of our respect and reverence":

> When we realize that every living thing and every aspect of the natural world, including ourselves, are a sacred part of divine conception, we are moved to live in a more reverential way . . . inspiring us to act in ways which cause the least harm and do the greatest good. . . . [A]ll of us, from every religious tradition, can still be touched by the sacred, numinous dimension of all Creation, which inspires us to live gently on the earth, with respect and reverence for all life.[102]

If we are to respect and revere all life, as Fox says, it is our task "to live and let live . . . and to love all and serve all. . . ." These simple actions are "the basic elements of a humane society, and of a sustainable and just global community."[103]

We must begin by changing our institutionalized cruelty towards and exploitation of creatures that are not human, subjecting them to unprovoked attack—on the land, in the air, and under the sea—for our amusement, profit, and convenience. We must learn to cherish nature and its life forms, not destroy them. Otherwise, a global calamity may befall us, devastating our human society not with one big action, but with many small ones.

A humane, sustainable society, that is decent and compassionate towards its least empowered members, is essential to our own long-term survival and prosperity. It is our only hope. If we do not soon learn this, we will suffer the consequences.

CREDITS

Excerpt on page 21 is from *Cosmos*, by Carl Sagan © 1980 by Carl Sagan. Used by permission of The Estate of Carl Sagan.

Excerpt on page 38 is reprinted with the permission of The Globe Newspaper Company, from "Chilling Evidence of Climactic Meltdown," by Ross Gelbspan, which appeared in the January 21, 2000 edition of *The Boston Globe*. Permission conveyed through Copyright Clearance Center.

Excerpt on page 54 is from "After the Storm, An Ecological Bomb," by William K. Stevens, which appeared in the November 30, 1999 edition of *The New York Times*. Copyright © 2000 by The New York Times Co. Reprinted by permission.

Excerpt on page 55 is from "Failing our Farmers," by Wendell Berry, which appeared in the July 6, 1999 edition of *The New York Times*. Copyright © 2000 by The New York Times Co. Reprinted by permission.

Excerpt on page 80 is from *A Sand County Almanac* by Aldo Leopold © 1966. Used by permission of Oxford University Press, NY.

Excerpt on pages 89 and 90 is reprinted with the permission of The Globe Newspaper Company, from "She was chewing off her paw

NOTES

Chapter 1. Loving Animals for Their Own Sake

1. John A. Hoyt, personal communication, December 1999.

2. Georges Seldes, *The Great Quotations* (New York: Pocket Books, 1970), pp. 281–282.

3. William Edward Hartpole Lecky, *History of European Morals*, Vol. 2 (New York: Arno Viers, 1975), Chap. 4.

4. Michael W. Fox, *Saint Francis of Assisi, Animals, and Nature*, Part I (Washington, DC: The Humane Society of the United States, 1989).

5. Saint Francis of Assisi, *The Little Flowers of St. Francis* (New York: E. P. Dutton, 1951), pp. 36–54.

6. Lewis G. Regenstein, "The Early Christian Saints," in *Replenish the Earth* (New York: Crossroad, 1991), Chap. 3.

7. Ann Cottrell Free, *Animals, Nature, and Albert Schweitzer* (Washington, DC: Flying Fox Press, 1988).

8. Ibid.

9. Ibid.

10. Cleveland Amory, *ManKind? Our Incredible War on Wildlife* (New York: Harper & Row, 1974), pp. 77–78.

11. Richard Cartwright Austin, *Baptized Into the Wilderness: A Christian Perspective on John Muir* (John Knox Press, 1987), pp. 8–9.

12. Robert McConnell Hatch, "Cornerstones for a Conservation Ethic," *Atlantic Naturalist*, April–June l967, p. 155.

13. Ibid.

14. Robert McConnell Hatch, "Conservation: A Challenge to the Churches," *Appalachia*, Appalachian Mountain Club, Boston, June l968, pp. 22–24.

15. Andrew Linzey, "The Place of Animals in Creation: A Christian View," in *Animal Sacrifices: Religious Perspectives on the Use of Animals in Science*, ed, Tom Regan (Philadelphia: Temple University Press), pp. 115–148.

16. Ibid.

17. Michael W. Fox, *The Boundless Circle* (Wheaton, IL.: Quest Books, 1996), pp. 204, 261–265.

18. Charles G. Spencer, "The Fulfillment of Life," *Earth Ethics*, Center for Respect of Life and Environment, Washington, DC, Fall/Winter l997–1998, pp. 7–9.

19. John A. Hoyt, "The Rights of Animals," *Earth Ethics*, Center for Respect of Life and Environment, Washington, DC, Spring/Summer l996, pp. 22–23.

20. John Hart, "Spirituality in Creation: The Life and Teachings of Francis of Assisi," *Earth Ethics*, Center for Respect of Life and Environment, Washington, DC, Fall 1996, pp. 4–5.

21. Ibid.

22. "Animals, Cruelty to," *Encyclopedia Judaica* (Jerusalem: Keter, l974), pp. 6–7.

23. Ibid.

24. "Animals, Protection of," *Universal Jewish Encyclopedia* (New York, 1939).

25. Karan Singh, "The Hindu Declaration on Nature," in *Hinduism: The Kinship of All Creatures*, Lewis Regenstein.

26. John B. Noss, *Man's Religions* (New York: Macmillan, l966), pp. 154–168.

27. Michael Tobias, "Ahimsa," *The Animals' Voice*, Los Angeles, 1989, p. 57.

28. Lewis G. Regenstein, "Jainism: Never Harm Any Living Creature," in *Replenish the Earth*, Chap. 13, op. cit.

29. Michael W. Fox, personal communication, January 2000.

30. V.A. Holmes-Gore, *These We Have Not Loved* (Wheaton, IL: Theosophical Press, 1946), p. 6.

31. Chatsumarn Kabilsingh, "How Buddhism Can Help Protect Nature," in *Tree of Life: Buddhism and Protection of Nature*, Peter Scott (Hong Kong: Geneva Buddhist Perception of Nature, 1987), p. 11.

32. Lewis G. Regenstein, "Buddhism: Compassion for All Creatures," in *Replenish the Earth*, Chap. 14, op. cit.

33. Abou Bakr Ahmed Ba Kader, Abdul Latif Tawfik El Shirazy Al Sabbagh, Mohammed Al Sayyed Al Glenid, and Movel Yousef Samarrai Izzidian, *Islamic Principles for Conservation of the Natural Environment* (Gland, Switzerland: International Union for the Conservation of Nature and Natural Resources, 1983), pp. 16–17.

34. Ibid.

35. Michael W. Fox, *The Boundless Circle*, op. cit., p. 266.

36. E.S. Turner, *All Heaven in a Rage* (New York: St. Martin's Press, 1965), p. 12.

37. Stephen Jay Gould, "The Human Difference," Op-Ed Page, *The New York Times*, July 2, 1999.

38. Charles Darwin, *The Descent of Man* (Princeton, NJ: Princeton University Press, 1981).

39. Michael W. Fox, *The Boundless Circle*, op. cit.

40. Carl Sagan, *Cosmos* (New York: Ballantine Books, 1980), p. 236.

41. "Preserving and Cherishing the Earth," An Appeal for Joint Commitment in Science and Religion; Statement of Scientists; Response of Religious Leaders; January 1990; from Carl Sagan, Cornell University, Ithaca, New York.

42. John A. Hoyt, *Animals in Peril* (Garden City Park, NY: Avery Publishing Group, 1994).

43. *Sabbath Newsletter*, United Nations Environment Program, New York, June 1990, p. 4.

44. John A. Hoyt, "Secular Spirituality," *Earth Ethics*, Center for Respect of Life and Environment, Washington, DC, Fall/Winter 1997–1998, p. 6.

45. Vincent Rossi, "The Eleventh Commandment: Toward an Ethic of Ecology," *Epiphany Journal*, San Francisco, 1981.

46. "Preserving and Cherishing the Earth," op. cit.

47. John A. Hoyt, "The 1998 International Albert Schweitzer Lecture," Address at Yale University, October 7, 1998.

48. Michael W. Fox, *Inhumane Society* (New York: St. Martin's Press, 1999), p. 125.

49. Thomas Berry, *The Universe Story* (San Francisco: Harper, 1994), pp. 3–5.

50. Thomas Berry, *The Dream of the Earth* (San Francisco: Sierra Club Books, 1988), p. xv.

51. Jan Hartke, personal communication, January 2000.

52. Michael W. Fox, *The Boundless Circle*, op. cit., p. 61.

53. Thomas Berry, *The Universe Story*, op. cit.

54. Ibid.

Chapter 2. Are We Killing Our Planet?

1. Christopher Flavin, Worldwatch Institute, Washington, DC, "Earth Matters," CNN, January 17, 1999.

2. "World Scientists' Warning to Humanity," Union of Concerned Scientists, Cambridge, Massachusetts, November 18, 1992.

3. Ibid.

4. Lester R. Brown, et al., *Vital Signs 1999: The Environmental Trends That Are Shaping Our Future* (New York: W.W. Norton, 1999), p. 11.

5. United Nations Population Division and U.S. Census Bureau, from "Six Billion and Counting," *The New York Times*, September 19, 1999, p. wk5.

6. "The Global Environment and Basic Human Needs," President's Council on Environmental Quality, Washington, DC, 1978.

7. Paul Lewis, "World Bank Says Poverty Is Increasing," *The New York Times*, June 3, 1999; David Briscoe, Associated Press, "Ranks of Poor Rising in Wake of Global Financial Crisis," *The Atlanta Journal and Constitution*, June 3, 1999, p. A18.

8. Lester Brown, et al., *State of the World 1999* (New York: W.W. Norton, 1999), p. 20.

9. *Human Development Report 1998*, United Nations Development Program, New York, 1998.

10. "Pop Quiz: Who's Consuming the Planet?" The Pew Global Stewardship Initiative, *The New York Times*, April 18, 1994.

11. Ibid.

12. *Human Development Report 1998*, op. cit., p.2.

13. Ibid.

14. Barbara Crossette, "Most Consuming More, and the Rich Much More," *The New York Times*, September 13, 1998.

15. William K. Stevens, "Global Temperatures At a High for the First 5 Months of 1998," *The New York Times*, 1998, pp. A1, A16.

16. Seth Dunn, "Wealth-Related Losses Hit New High," in *Vital Signs1999*, op. cit.

17. Lester Brown, et al., *State of the World 1999*, op. cit.

18. Ibid.

19. Ibid.

20. Ibid.

21. Larry Rohter, "Venezuela Struggles to Calculate Toll From Floods and Mudslides," *The New York Times*, December 21, 1999, p. A16.

22. William K. Stevens, "1999 Continues Warming Trend Around Globe," *The New York Times*, December 19, 1999, pp. 1, 18.

23. Suzanne Daley, "France: Toll on Trees," World Briefing, *The New York Times*, January 5, 2000, p. A6.

24. Steve Newman, "EarthWeek: A Diary of the Planet," Science Section, *The Atlanta Journal and Constitution*, January 2000.

25. Lester Brown, et al., *State of the World 1999*, op. cit.

26. Charles J. Hanley, Associated Press, "Islands Tell of Losing Their

Land to the Sea," *The Atlanta Journal and Constitution*, June 25, 1997, p. A9.

27. Ibid.

28. "Clinton, at U.N., Defers Curbs on Gases Warming the Globe," *The New York Times*, June 27, 1997, p. A7.

29. Steve Newman, "EarthWeek: A Diary of the Planet," *The Atlanta Journal and Constitution*, June 20, 1999.

30. William K. Stevens, "Global Temperatures At a High for the First 5 Months of 1998," op. cit.

31. William K. Stevens, "1999 Continues Warming Trend Around Globe," op. cit.

32. Ross Gelbspan, "Chilling Evidence of Climatic Meltdown," *Boston Globe*, January 21, 2000.

33. "Scientific Assessment of Ozone Depletion: 1994—Executive Summary," National Oceanic and Atmospheric Administration, National Aeronautics and Space Administration, United Nations Environment Program, World Meteorological Organization; U.S. Environmental Protection Agency, Washington, DC, February 1995.

34. "Stratospheric Update," U.S. Environmental Protection Agency, Washington, DC, September 1997.

35. "Fact Sheet. Summary of Proposed Regulations for Recycling of Substitute Refrigerants Under Section 608," U.S. Environmental Protection Agency, Washington, DC, June 1998.

36. Reuters, "Ozone Hole Reported to Be Biggest Yet Seen," *The New York Times*, October 7, 1998.

37. "Estimated New Cancer Cases and Deaths by Sex for All Sites, United States, 1999," *Cancer Facts & Figures 1999*, American Cancer Society, Atlanta, Georgia.

38. John H. Cushman, Jr., "Peach Oil May Work as Pesticide," *The New York Times*, March 14, 1999.

39. Meredith McGehee and Celia Wexler, "While Nation Stewed, Special Interests Quietly Got Their Way," *The Atlanta Constitution*, Op-Ed Page, n.d.

40. Jeff Nesmith, "Proposed Law Would Slash Production of Chemicals," *The Atlanta Constitution*, 1986; Lewis G. Regenstein, *Clean-*

ing Up America the Poisoned (Washington, DC: Acropolis Books, 1993), p. 205.

41. Lester Brown, et al., *State of the World 1999,* op. cit.

42. "1997 National Resources Inventory: Highlights," USDA Natural Resources Conservation Service, Athens, Georgia, December 1999.

43. Walter V. Reid and Kenton R. Miller, *Keeping Options Alive,* World Resources Institute, Washington, DC, 1989, pp. 37–38.

44. Robert Constanza, et al., "The Value of the World's Ecosystem Services and Natural Capital," *Nature,* May 15, 1997, pp. 253–259.

45. Ibid.

46. Lester Brown, et al. *State of the World 1999,* op. cit., p. 11.

47. Ibid.

48. Theodore Dalrymple, "Taking Good Health for Granted," *The Wall Street Journal,* Editorial Page, March 31, 1999.

49. Philip J. Hilts, "Life at 100 Is Surprisingly Healthy," *The New York Times,* June 1999, p. D7.

50. John Tuxill, "Appreciating the Benefits of Plant Diversity," in *State of the World 1999* (Washington, DC: Worldwatch Institute, 1999), p. 97.

51. Associated Press, "Clinton Decries Huge Food Waste," *The Atlanta Journal and Constitution,* n.d.

52. "Estimated New Cancer Cases and Death by Sex for All Sites," op. cit.

53. Paul R. Epstein, "Overview," in *Climate Changes* (Washington, DC: World Wildlife Fund, July 1996).

54. Ibid.

55. Thomas Berry, personal communication, 1998.

Chapter 3. The Demise of American Agriculture

1. Gary L. Valen, "Agribusiness: Farming Without Culture," The Humane Society of the United States, Washington, DC, May 23, 1999.

2. Robert F. Welborn, "Quality Agriculture," *Earth Ethics,* Center for

Respect of Life and Environment, Washington, DC, Spring/Summer, 1998, pp. 19–20.

3. Wendell Berry, "Failing Our Farmers," *The New York Times*, Op-Ed Page, July 6, 1999.

4. Gary L. Valen, "Life on the Factory Farm," *HSUS News*, The Humane Society of the United States, Washington, DC, Winter 1999, p. 17.

5. Melanie Adcock, "The Real Price of Factory Farming," The Humane Society of the United States, Washington, DC, Winter 1998, pp. 1–6.

6. Ibid.

7. Dan Looker, "Hog Farm Revolutionary," *HSUS News*, The Humane Society of the United States, Washington, DC, Winter 1999, pp. 14–17.

8. Gary L. Valen, "Life on the Factory Farm," op. cit.

9. Melanie Adcock, op. cit.

10. David Barboza, "Is the Sun Setting on Farmers?" Business Section, *The Sunday New York Times*, November 28, 1999, pp. 1, 14.

11. Gary L. Valen, "Life on the Factory Farm," op. cit.

12. Michael W. Fox, *Inhumane Society* (New York: St. Martin's Press, 1990).

13. Michael W. Fox, *Eating With Conscience: The Bioethics of Food* (Troutdale, OR: New Sage Press, 1997), pp. 11–14, 52, 166.

14. "Animal Agriculture Claims Record Number of Victims," "The Farm Report," Farm Animal Reform Movement, Bethesda, Maryland, Summer/Fall 1995.

15. Melanie Adcock, op. cit.

16. Gary L. Valen, "Life on the Factory Farm," op. cit.

17. "Choosing a Humane Diet: How to Get Started," The Humane Society of the United States, Washington, DC, 1998.

18. Melanie Adcock, op. cit.

19. Stanley Dundon, "Charter for a Shared Farming Ethic," *Earth Ethics*, Spring/Summer 1998, pp. 6–7.

20. "Creating a New Vision of Farming: A Production Ethic for the

Twenty-First Century," Soul of Agriculture Project, Center for Respect of Life and Environment, Washington, DC, October 1998.

21. Wendell Berry, op. cit.

22. Ibid.

23. Michael W. Fox, *Eating With Conscience*, op. cit.

24. David Barboza, op. cit.

25. Richard M. Clugston, "Sustainability and Rural Revitalization: Two Alternative Visions," in *Rural Sustainable Development in America*, ed. Ivonne Audirac (New York: John Wiley & Sons, 1996).

26. David Barboza, op. cit.

27. Richard M. Clugston, op. cit.

28. Ibid.

29. Melanie Adcock, op. cit.

30. Mike Wallace, "Big Chicken," *60 Minutes*, December 19, 1999.

31. Melanie Adcock, op. cit.

32. Scott Montgomery and Elliott Jaspin, "Deadly New Forms of E. coli Invade U.S. Food Supply," *The Atlanta Journal and Constitution*, December 12, 1999, pp. A1, A20.

33. Denise Grady, "A Move to Limit Antibiotic Use in Animal Feed," *The New York Times*, March 8, 1999, pp. A1, A13.

34. Denise Grady, "Bacteria Cases in Denmark Cause Antibiotics Concerns in U.S.," *The New York Times*, November 4, 1999, p. A15.

35. Paul Duggan, "U.S. Court's Ruling Blocks New Rules on Meat Safety," *The Washington Post*, December 11, 1999.

36. "Play the Food Safety Lottery: Odds Are One in Four You'll Get Sick this Year," Center for Science in the Public Interest, Washington, DC, September 16, 1999.

37. "Fighting Factory Farms," *Humane Activist*, The Humane Society of the United States, Washington, DC, September/October 1999.

38. Denise Grady, "A Move to Limit Antibiotic Use in Animal Feed," op. cit.

39. Ibid.

40. Ibid.

41. Michael W. Fox, personal communication, December 27, 1999.

42. Ibid.

43. Associated Press, "More Soy, Less Fat on School Menus," *The Atlantic Constitution*, March 10, 2000, p. A 12.

44. Ed Ayres, "Beyond 2000 Will We Still Eat Meat?" *Time*, November 8, 1999.

45. Melanie Adcock, op. cit.

46. Pamela Rice, "Everything You Never Wanted to Know About Manure," *Vegetarian Voice*, The North American Vegetarian Society, Dolgeville, New York, Fall 1999, p. 8.

47. Melanie Adcock, op. cit.

48. Ibid.

49. Ibid.

50. Michele Nowlin, "Should North Carolina Allow More Hogs to Be Slaughtered?" *The Wall Street Journal*, February 3, 1999, p. S4.

51. Melanie Adcock, op. cit.

52. Ibid.

53. Liz Murray, "Dead Zone Hit Record in the Gulf, " *The New York Times*, December 14, 1999.

54. Michele Nowlin, op. cit.

55. William K. Stevens, "After the Storm, an Ecological Bomb," *The New York Times*, November 30, 1999, pp. F1–F2.

56. Marlon Manuel, "Fear Spreads on Dirty N.C. Water," *The Atlanta Journal and Constitution*, September 26, 1999, pp. A1, A17.

57. Peter Kilborn, "Storm Highlights Flaws in Farm Law in North Carolina," *The New York Times*, October 17, 1999, pp. 1, 26.

58. "HSUS Says New Report Highlights Need for Changes in American Agriculture," The Humane Society of the United States, Washington, DC, December 23, 1999.

59. William K. Stevens, op. cit.

60. Michele Nowlin, op. cit.

61. Wendell Berry, op. cit.

62. Al Gore, "Inside Politics," CNN, December 23, 1999.

63. Melanie Adcock, op. cit.

64. Karen Lundegaard and Esther M. Bauer, "Texan Questions Future of N.C.'s Hog Industry," *The Wall Street Journal*, December 1, 1999.

65. "Environmental Protection Ranks High With Iowa Voters," League of Conservation Voters Education Fund, Washington, DC, Fall 1999.

66. "Fighting Factory Farms," op. cit.

67. Daniel Akst, "Don't Coddle Farmers, Buy Them Out," Sunday Business Section, *The New York Times*, n.d.

68. Gary L. Valen, "Agribusiness: Farming Without Culture," op. cit.

69. "Can Industrial Agriculture Feed the World?" Turning Point Project, *The New York Times*, January 18, 2000, p. A13.

70. "Biotechnology-Hunger," Turning Point Project, *The New York Times*, November 8, 1999, p. A5.

71. Gary L. Valen, "Agribusiness: Farming Without Culture," op. cit.

72. Linda Elswick, personal communication, December 14, 1999.

73. Neal D. Barnard, "World Bank's Aim: Beef for China," *The New York Times*, Op-Ed Page, December 28, 1999.

74. Andrew Pollack, "Talks on BioTech Food Today in Montreal Will See U.S. Isolated," *The New York Times*, January 24, 1999, p. A10.

75. "Who Plays G*d in the Twenty-First Century?" Turning Point Project, *The New York Times*, October 11, 1999, p. A11.

76. "Genetic Roulette," Turning Point Project, *The New York Times*, October 26, 1999, p. A15.

77. "Unlabeled, Untested . . . and You're Eating It," Turning Point Project, *The New York Times*, October 18, 1999, p. A13.

78. Ibid.

79. Gina Kolata, "Scientists Place Jellyfish Genes Into Monkeys," *The New York Times*, December 23, 1999, pp. A1, A20.

80. Michael W. Fox, "The Cloning Controversy: After Dolly, Are

Animal Factories Next?" *HSUS News*, The Humane Society of the United States, Washington, DC, Summer 1997, pp. 11–14.

81. "Genetic Roulette," op. cit.

82. "Biotechnology-Hunger," op. cit.

83. Frederick Kirschenmann, "Dancing With Nature: An Emerging Ethic for Sustainable Agriculture," *Earth Ethics*, Spring 1993, pp. 1, 5.

84. Carol Kaesuk Yoon, "Altered Corn May Imperil Butterfly, Researchers Say," *The New York Times*, n.d., pp. A1, A20.

85. Carol Kaesuk Yoon, "No Consensus on the Effects of Altered Corn on Butterflies," *The New York Times*, November 3, 1999.

86. Frederick Golden, "Of Corn and Butterflies," *Time*, May 31, 1999, pp. 80–81.

87. Ibid.

88. Carol Kaesuk Yoon, "No Consensus on the Effects of Altered Corn on Butterflies" op. cit.

89. Carol Kaesuk Yoon, "Altered Corn May Imperil Butterfly, Researchers Say," op. cit.

90. Marian Burros, "U.S. Plans Long-Term Studies on Safety of Genetically Altered Foods," *The New York Times*, July 14, 1999, p. A16.

91. Sheryl Gay Stolberg, "New Information on Gene Patient's Death Fails to Resolve Mystery," *The New York Times*, December 1, 1999.

92. Marian Burros, op. cit.

93. Melody Petersen, "New Trade Threat for U.S. Farmers," *The New York Times*, August 28, 1999.

94. Ibid.

95. Marian Burros, op. cit.

96. Barnaby J. Feder, "Rocky Outlook for Genetically Engineered Crops," *The New York Times*, January 2000.

97. Andrew Pollack, "A Disputed Study Suggests Possible Harm From Genetically Altered Food," *The New York Times*, October 15, 1999, p. A19.

98. Ibid.

99. Ibid.

100. Marian Burros, op. cit.

101. "Unlabeled, Untested . . . and You're Eating It," op. cit.

102. "Biotechnology-Hunger," op. cit.

103. "Victory!! Monsanto Dumps 'Terminator' Technology !" Global Response Action Status, Environmental Action and Education Network, December 1999.

104. Scott Kilman, "Monsanto Won't Commercialize Terminator Gene," *The Wall Street Journal*, n.d.

105. Michael W. Fox, "The Cloning Controversy: After Dolly, Are Animal Factories Next?" op. cit.

106. Michael W. Fox, personal communication, op. cit.

107. Colin Tudge, *The Time Before History: 5 Million Years of Human Impact* (A Touchstone Book, 1996), pp. 265–279.

108. Jeremy Rifkin, "Big Bad Beef," *The New York Times*, Op-Ed Page, March 23, 1992.

109. W.C. Lowdermilk, "Conquest of the Land Through 7,000 Thousand Years," Agriculture Information Bulletin No. 99, U.S. Department of Agriculture, Soil Conservation Service, August 1989.

110. Ibid.

111. Ed Ayres, op. cit.

112. Ibid.

113. "Choosing a Humane Diet: How to Get Started," op. cit.

114. "Vision Statement/Call to Action: Building a New Ethic of Production in Agriculture," The Soul of Agriculture National Conference, Minneapolis, Minnesota, November 1997.

115. Gita M. Smith, "Georgia Third in Loss of Green Space to Sprawl," *The Atlanta Journal and Constitution*, December 7, 1999, p. A12.

116. "1997 National Resources Inventory: Highlights," USDA Natural Resources Conservation Service, Athens, Georgia, December 1999.

117. Ibid.

118. Gita M. Smith, op. cit.

119. Daniel Hillel, *Out of the Earth: Civilization and the Life of the Soil* (California: University of California Press, 1992).

120. "Can Industrial Agriculture Feed the World?" Turning Point Project, *The New York Times*, January 18, 2000, p. A13.

121. Paul and Anne Ehrlich, *Extinction: The Causes and Consequences of the Disappearance of Species* (New York: Random House, 1981).

122. Jan Hartke, personal communication, January 2000.

123. Frederick Kirschenmann, op. cit.

124. Ibid.

125. Richard M. Clugston, op. cit.

126. Terry Gips, Melanie Adcock, and Ellen Truong, "The Humane Consumer and Producer Guide," The Humane Society of the United States and the International Alliance for Sustainable Agriculture, Washington, DC., 1993.

127. Richard M. Clugston, op. cit.

128. "Vision Statement/Call to Action," op. cit.

129. Ibid.

130. Ibid.

131. Ibid.

132. Dan Looker, op. cit.

133. Wendell Berry, op. cit.

134. Thomas Berry, "The Challenge of Our Times," *Earth Ethics*, Center for Respect of Life and Environment, Washington, DC, Fall/Winter 1997–1998, pp. 29, 32.

135. Ibid.

136. Richard M. Clugston, op. cit.

137. Robert F. Welborn, op. cit.

Chapter 4. Hunting—Sport or Slaughter?

1. Susan Hagood, "Hunters' Privilege," *HSUS News*, The Humane Society of the United States, Washington, DC, Fall 1996, pp. 9–12.

2. Susan Hagood, "State Wildlife Management: The Pervasive Influence of Hunters, Hunting, and Money," The Humane Society of the United States, Washington, DC, February 1997, p. 10.

3. Ibid.

4. "Hunters' Privilege," op. cit.

5. "Learn the Facts about Hunting," The Humane Society of the United States, Washington, DC, 1997, pp. 9, 26–27.

6. James Fisher, et.al., *The Red Book: Wildlife in Danger* (New York: Viking Press, 1969), pp. 14–17.

7. Grover Krantz, "Human Activities and Megafaunal Extinctions," *American Scientist*, April 1970.

8. James Fisher, op. cit.

9. Thomas B. Allen, *Vanishing Wildlife of North America*, National Geographic Society, Washington, DC, 1975, pp. 16–26.

10. Ibid.

11. Grover Krantz, op. cit.

12. Thomas B. Allen, op. cit.

13. "Maine Fish and Game," Maine Department of Wildlife, Winter 1972–1973; from Lewis Regenstein, *The Politics of Extinction* (New York: Macmillan, 1975), pp. 6–7.

14. Mitch Snow, "Hunters, Anglers, and Boaters Provide $378 Million for Sports Fish and Wildlife Restoration Programs," U.S. Fish and Wildlife Service, Washington, DC, March 19, 1999.

15. "Draft Environmental Impact Statement, Federal Aid in Fish and Wildlife Restoration Program," Appendix I-C, Table 1-A; "Current and Projected Program Activity Levels of the Federal Aid Program," U.S. Department of the Interior, Fish and Wildlife Service, Washington, DC, 1975.

16. Ibid.

17. *1996 National Survey of Fishing, Hunting, and Wildlife-Associated Recreation*, U.S. Department of the Interior, Fish and Wildlife Service, and U.S. Department of Commerce, Bureau of the Census, 1996, pp. 4–6.

18. John A. Hoyt, *Animals in Peril* (Garden City Park, NY: Avery Publishing Group, 1994), p. 195.

19. Elizabeth Boo, *Ecotourism: The Potentials and Pitfalls*, Vol. I (Washington, DC: World Wildlife Fund, 1990), p. 16.

20. Lewis Regenstein, *The Politics of Extinction* (New York: Harper & Row, 1974), p. 77.

21. Aldo Leopold, *A Sand County Almanac* (New York: Ballantine Books, 1966).

22. "Learn the Facts about Hunting," op. cit.

23. Ibid.

24. Ibid.

25. Ibid.

26. Ibid.

27. Ibid.

28. Lewis Regenstein, op. cit.

29. "Killing Their Childhood: How Public Schools and Government Agencies Are Promoting Sport Hunting to America's Children," The Fund for Animals, New York, December 1997, pp. 2, 9, 11.

30. Ibid.

31. Ibid.

32. Ibid.

33. Patrick Reilly, "Venerable Hunting Magazine Disarms, Tries Kayaking," *The Wall Street Journal*, July 6, 1999, pp. A17, A20.

34. Ibid.

35. "Killing their Childhood," op. cit.

36. "Learn the Facts about Hunting," op. cit.

Chapter 5. Trapping—Legalized Torture of Animals

1. Cathy Liss, "Trapping and Poisoning," *Animals and their Legal Rights* (Washington, DC: Animal Welfare Institute, 1990), Chap. 10, pp. 157–189.

2. Travis Ryan, "A Heinous, Barbaric Device," *Making a Difference for Animals* (Washington, DC: The Humane Society of the United States, 1996), Chap. 13, pp. 109–110.

3. Cathy Liss, op. cit.

4. Ibid.

5. Ibid.

6. Travis Ryan, op. cit.

7. Tom Garrett, personal communication, 1972.

8. Cathy Liss and Christine Stevens, "Opposition to Steel Jaw Leghold Traps Is Overwhelming," Animal Welfare Institute, Washington, DC, December 2, 1996.

9. Scot Leigh, "She was chewing off her paw to try to break free," *The Boston Globe*, October 22, 1995; as reprinted in *The Animal Welfare Institute (AWI) Quarterly*, Washington, DC, Fall 1995, p. 2.

10. Ibid.

11. James P. Sterba, "A Montana Trapper Hangs On to a Calling Most Love to Hate," *The Wall Street Journal*, June 28, 1999, pp. A1, A6.

12. Thomas B. Allen, *Vanishing Wildlife of North America*, National Geographic Society, Washington, DC, 1975, pp. 12–16.

13. James P. Sterba, op. cit.

14. Ibid.

15. Thomas B. Allen, op. cit.

16. Dale Bartlett, The Humane Society of the United States, personal communication, April 7, 1997.

17. Ibid.

18. Cathy Liss, "Trapping and Poisoning," op. cit.

19. Matthew Scully, "The Last Gasps of the Fur Trade," *HSUS News*, The Humane Society of the United States, Washington, DC, Fall 1998, pp. 16–22.

20. "An Initiative to Stop Wolf Snaring in Alaska," *Action Line*, Friends of Animals, Darien, CT, Winter 1997–1998, pp. 12–15.

21. Ibid.

22. Danielle Bays, "Is Fur Really 'Back'?" *HSUS News*, The Humane Society of the United States, Washington, DC, Winter 1998, pp.10–11.

23. Ibid.

24. Matthew Scully, op. cit.

25. Patricia Forkan, personal communication, December 1999.

26. Danielle Bays, op. cit.

27. Matthew Scully, op. cit.

28. "Betrayal of Trust: The slaughter of dogs and cats is the fur industry's ugly secret," *HSUS News,* The Humane Society of the United States, Washington, DC, Winter 1998, pp. 19–21.

29. Ibid.

30. Travis Ryan, op. cit.

31. Ibid.

32. Patricia Wolff, "The City Slicker's Guide to Welfare Ranching in New Mexico," *Wildlife Tracks,* The Humane Society of the United States, Washington, DC, Fall 1998.

33. Dale Bartlett, op. cit.

34. James P. Sterba, op. cit.

35. James Brooke, "Lethal Virus Borne by Mice Makes Return in the West," *The New York Times,* June 25, 1998.

36. "Hantavirus upswing," *The Atlanta Constitution,* June 12, 1998.

37. Robert Bazell, *NBC Nightly News,* June 22, 1999.

38. Cathy Liss, "Trapping and Poisoning," op. cit.

39. Danielle Bays, op. cit.

40. Matthew Scully, op. cit.

41. Ibid.

42. "Trapping in the United States," Animal Welfare Institute, Washington, DC.

43. Cathy Liss and Christine Stevens, op. cit.

44. "Trapping in the United States," op. cit.

45. Ibid.

46. Travis Ryan, op. cit.

47. Matthew Scully, op. cit.

48. Patricia Forkan, op. cit.

49. Christine Stevens, "Let the Administration Know How You Feel about Leghold Traps," *The Animal Welfare Institute (AWI) Quarterly,* Washington, DC, Winter 1996, p. 4.

50. Cathy Liss, "Trapping and Poisoning," op. cit.

51. Danielle Bays, op. cit.

52. Matthew Scully, op. cit.

53. Cathy Liss, "Trapping and Poisoning," op. cit.

54. Matthew Scully, "A Designer's Evolution," *HSUS News,* The Humane Society of the United States, Washington, DC, Fall 1998, p. 23.

55. Lewis G. Regenstein, *The Politics of Extinction* (New York: Macmillan, 1975), p. 120.

56. John Paradiso, "Status Report on Cats of the World," U.S. Department of the Interior, Fish and Wildlife Service, Office of Endangered Species, Washington, DC, 1971.

57. Matthew Scully, "A Designer's Evolution," op. cit.

58. Ibid.

59. Danielle Bays, "HSUS Launches Fur-Free 2000," *HSUS News,* The Humane Society of the United States, Washington, DC, Fall 1998, p. 20.

60. Danielle Bays, "Is Fur Really 'Back'?" op. cit.

Chapter 6. Species Extinction and the Threat to Humanity

1. Walter V. Reid and Kenton R. Miller, *Keeping Options Alive: The Scientific Basis for Conserving Biodiversity,* World Resources Institute, Washington, DC, 1989, pp. 37–38.

2. Edward O. Wilson, "Is Humanity Suicidal? We're Flirting with the Extinction of Our Species," *The New York Times Magazine,* May 30, 1993.

3. Lewis G. Regenstein, "Extinction," *The Environmental Encyclopedia* (Detroit: Gale Research, 1998), pp. 395–396.

4. Malcolm W. Browne, "Living on Borrowed Time," *The New York Times Book Review,* December 15, 1991, pp. 7–9.

5. Lewis G. Regenstein, op. cit.

6. Colin Tudge, *Last Animals at the Zoo: How Mass Extinctions Can be Stopped* (Washington, DC: Island Press, 1992).

7. David M. Raup, *Extinction: Bad Genes, or Bad Luck?* (New York: W.W. Norton, 1991).

8. Walter V. Reid and Kenton R. Miller, op. cit.

9. William K. Stevens, "One in Every 8 Plant Species is Imperiled, a Survey Finds," *The New York Times*, April 9, 1998, pp. A1, A22.

10. Peter H. Raven, "Endangered Realm," in *The Emerald Realm*, National Geographic Society, Washington, DC, 1990.

11. *Global 2000 Report to the President*, U.S. Department of State and President's Council on Environmental Quality, Washington, DC, 1980.

12. Walter V. Reid and Kenton R. Miller, op. cit., p. 15.

13. Erik Eckholm, *Disappearing Species: The Social Challenge*, Worldwatch Institute, Washington, DC, July 1978.

14. Edward O. Wilson, *Consilience: The Unity of Knowledge* (New York: Knopf, 1998) pp. 292–293.

15. "Noah's Ark is Leaking: The Department of Interior Abandons International Species protection," PEER White Paper, Public Employees for Environmental Responsibility, Washington, DC, May 1997.

16. Tom Teepen, "With every leap, you must prepare a landing," *The Atlanta Constitution*, May 25, 1999, p. A11.

17. Erik Eckholm, op. cit.

18. *The Global Environment and Basic Human Needs*, President's Council on Environmental Quality, Washington, DC, 1978.

19. Erik Eckholm, op. cit.

20. John Tuxill, "Appreciating the Benefits of Plant Biodiversity," *State of the World*, Worldwatch Institute, Washington, DC, 1999, pp. 96–114.

21. *The Global Environment and Basic Human Needs*, op. cit.

22. Edward O. Wilson, *Consilience*, op. cit.

23. *World Conservation Strategy Report*, United Nations Environment Program, New York, 1980.

24. *The Global Environment and Basic Human Needs,* op. cit.

25. John Tuxill, op. cit.

26. Edward O. Wilson, *Consilience,* op. cit.

27. William J. Broad, "The Diverse Creatures of the Deep May Be Starving," *The New York Times,* Science Section, June 1, 1999.

28. "War of Attrition: Sabotage of the Endangered Species Act by the U.S. Department of the Interior," PEER White Paper, Public Employees for Environmental Responsibility, Washington, DC, December 1997.

29. Ibid.

30. Ibid.

31. Ibid.

32. Ibid.

33. Ibid.

34. "Noah's Ark is Leaking: The Department of Interior Abandons International Species protection," op. cit.

35. Ibid.

36. Ibid.

37. Ibid.

38. Ibid.

39. U.S. Fish and Wildlife Service, "Retention of Threatened Status for the Continental Population of the African Elephant," *Federal Register,* August 10, 1992, p. 35,481.

40. Iain Douglas-Hamilton and Oria Douglas-Hamilton, *Battle for the Elephants* (New York: Viking Penguin, 1992), p. 338.

41. "Ban on Ivory Has Killed Demand in U.S., Study Finds," *The New York Times,* June 1990.

42. Jane Perlez, "Ban on Ivory Trading Is Reported to Force Cutbacks at Factories," *The New York Times,* May 22, 1990.

43. "Ivory Trade Renewed Despite Lack of Safeguards," *Humane Activist,* The Humane Society of the United States, Washington, DC, May–June, 1999.

44. "Noah's Ark is Leaking," op. cit.

45. Ibid., p. 23

46. Ibid., p. 17

47. Ibid., p. 23

48. Ibid., pp. 23–24

49. Ibid., p. 17

50. Ibid.

51. *1996 IUCN Red List of Threatened Animals*, World Conservation Union, Gland, Switzerland, 1996.

52. "Noah's Ark is Leaking," op. cit.

53. Ibid., p. 13

54. Ibid., p. 14

55. Ibid., pp. 6, 13

56. Norman Myers, *Gaia: An Atlas of Planet Management* (Garden City: NY: Anchor Press/Doubleday, 1984).

57. John Tuxill, *Losing Strands in the Web of Life: Vertebrate Declines and the Conservation of Biological Diversity*, Worldwatch Institute, Washington, DC, May 1998, pp. 9, 73.

58. George Small, *The Blue Whale* (New York: Columbia University Press, 1971).

59. Edward O. Wilson, "Is Humanity Suicidal?" op. cit.

60. John Tuxill, *Losing Strands in the Web of Life*, op. cit.

61. Norman Myers, op. cit.

Chapter 7. Sustainable Use or Unsustainable Slaughter?

1. Paul G. Irwin, Foreword in *Animals in Peril*, by John A. Hoyt (Garden City Park, NY: Avery Publishing Group, 1994).

2. "Tarnished Trophies," PEER White Paper, Public Employees for Environmental Responsibility, Washington, DC, October 1996, pp. 10–15.

3. Paul G. Irwin, op. cit.

4. Lee M. Talbot, "Principles for Living Resources Conservation," U.S. Marine Mammal Commission, Draft Preliminary Report on Consultations, Washington, DC, September 1993, p. 6.

5. Ronald M. Nowak, Comments submitted to the U.S. Fish and Wildlife Service on proposed rule to revise classification of the African elephant, July 10, 1991.

6. U.S. Fish and Wildlife Service, "Retention of Threatened Status for the Continental Population of the African Elephant," *Federal Register,* August 10, 1992, p. 35,481.

7. Iain Douglas-Hamilton and Oria Douglas-Hamilton, *Battle for the Elephants* (New York: Viking Penguin, 1992), p. 338.

8. "Ban on Ivory has Killed Demand in U.S., Study Finds," *The New York Times,* June 1990.

9. Jane Perlez, "Ban on Ivory Trading Is Reported to Force Cutbacks at Factories," *The New York Times,* May 22, 1990.

10. John A. Hoyt, *Animals in Peril* (Garden City Park, NY: Avery Publishing Group, 1994).

11. Philip Shabecoff, "Urgent Call from Wild to Boycott Ivory," *The New York Times,* May 15, 1988.

12. Raymond Bonner, "Crying Wolf Over Elephants," *The New York Times Magazine,* February 7, 1993.

13. Ronald M. Nowak, op. cit.

14. Wayne Pacelle, "Waste, Fraud, Abuse, and Animal Cruelty in Foreign Affairs Budget," The Humane Society of the United States, Washington, DC, February 10, 1997.

15. Wayne Pacelle, "Tax Dollars Fund Trophy Hunting," *HSUS News,* The Humane Society of the United States, Washington, DC, Fall 1997, pp. 7–8.

16. "Tarnished Trophies," op. cit.

17. Wayne Pacelle, "Tax Dollars Fund Trophy Hunting," op. cit.

18. U.S. Fish and Wildlife Service, "Proposed Endangered Status for Certain Populations of the African Elephant," *Federal Register,* March 18, 1991, pp. 11,392–11,393.

19. "Retention of Threatened Status for the Continental Population of the African Elephant," op. cit.

20. Ronald W. Nowak, op. cit.

21. "Ivory Trade Renewed Despite Lack of Safeguards," *Humane Activist,* The Humane Society of the United States, Washington, DC, May–June1999.

22. Roger Caras, *Last Chance on Earth,* Chilton, 1966; Donald G. McNeil, Jr., "Out of a Failed African Circus, a Lion of Legend," *The New York Times,* June 28, 1999.

23. "Filmmaker Claims Northern Botswana's Wildlife Is In Serious Decline; Blames Overhunting," *African Wildlife,* September–October 1993.

24. Dereck Joubert, "Report on the Hunting Concession Areas" Report to the Director of Wildlife, members of the Tawana Land Board, and the Office of the President of Botswana, 1993.

25. Matthew Scully, "Hunting for Fun and 'Charity'?" *The New York Times,* Op-Ed Page, April 17, 1999.

26. "Endangered Species Permit," *Federal Register,* December 12, 1978, p. 58, 121.

27. John H. Cushman, "Revising a Law Protecting Dolphins Divides Conservationists," *The New York Times,* March 14, 1994, p. A10.

28. "Hunting Lobby Takes Aim at Marine Mammal Protection Act," *Wildlife Watch,* April 1994, pp. 1, 8.

29. Ted Karasote, *Bloodties* (New York: Random House, 1993).

30. Ted Williams, "Open Season on Endangered Species," *Audubon,* January 1991.

31. Teresa M. Telecky and Doris Lin, "Trophy of Death," *HSUS News,* The Humane Society of the United States, Washington, DC, Fall 1995, pp. 27–31.

32. "Trophy Imports Out of Control," *Animal Activist Alert,* The Humane Society of the United States, Washington, DC, September 1995.

33. Teresa M. Telecky, op. cit.

34. Ibid.

35. Matthew Scully, op. cit.

36. "Tarnished Trophies," op. cit.

37. Ibid.

38. Teresa M. Telecky, op. cit.

39. Matthew Scully, op. cit.

40. Ibid.

41. Teresa M. Telecky, op. cit.

42. "Tarnished Trophies," op. cit.

43. Ibid.

44. Teresa M. Telecky, op. cit.

45. "Tarnished Trophies," op. cit.

46. Ibid.

47. Ibid.

48. Ibid.

49. Ibid.

50. Ibid.

51. John A. Hoyt, op. cit.

52. Richard Ellis, *The Book of Whales* (New York: Knopf, 1980), pp. 50–70.

53. Erich Hoyt, "Whale Watching Around the World," *International Whale Bulletin,* Summer 1992, pp. 1–8.

54. "Facts about the Wild Bird Trade"; "U.S. Importation Facts"; "Please Help Us Stop this Cruelty"; and "The Pet Trade in Wild Caught Birds"; The Humane Society of the United States, Washington, DC.

55. Charles H. Janson, "A Walk on the Wild Side," *Wildlife Conservation,* March–April 1994, p. 42.

56. John A. Hoyt, op. cit., p. 17.

57. Lee M. Talbot, op. cit.

58. Ibid.

59. Ibid.

60. Daniel Ludwig, Ray Hilborn, and Carl Watters, "Uncertainty, Resource Exploitation, and Conservation: Lessons from History," *Science,* April 2, 1995, pp. 17, 36.

61. Ibid.

62. Valerius Geist, "Wildlife Conservation as Wealth," *Nature,* April 7, 1994, pp. 491–492.

63. "Tarnished Trophies," op. cit., p. 7.

64. John A. Hoyt, op. cit.

65. Ibid.

66. Ibid., p. 3

Chapter 8. Towards a Humane Society

1. Michael W. Fox, *Inhumane Society* (New York: St. Martin's Press, 1990), pp. 73, 249.

2. Bernard Unte, "The Humane Prospect: Creating a Compassionate Society" (unpublished paper, 1999).

3. Dr. Randall Lockwood and Guy R. Hodge, "The Tangled Web of Animal Abuse: The Links Between Cruelty to Animals and Human Violence," *The Humane Society News*, The Humane Society of the United States, Washington, DC, Summer 1986.

4. Dr. Randall Lockwood, Statement Before Georgia Legislative Committee on Animal Cruelty Bill, Atlanta, Georgia, November 4, 1999.

5. Dr. Randall Lockwood, "Deadly Serious: An FBI Perspective on Animal Cruelty," *HSUS News*, The Humane Society of the United States, Washington, DC, Fall 1996.

6. "Violence to Humans and Animals: An Important Link," American Humane Association, Englewood, Colorado, November 1997.

7. Ibid.

8. Ibid.

9. Ibid.

10. "Youth Violence and Animal Cruelty," First Strike Campaign, The Humane Society of the United States, Washington, DC, May 1999.

11. Dr. Randall Lockwood and Guy R. Hodge, op. cit.

12. Ibid.

13. "Violence to Humans and Animals," op. cit.

14. "Youth Violence and Animal Cruelty," op. cit.

15. "Violence to Humans and Animals," op. cit.

16. "Youth Violence and Animal Cruelty," op. cit.

17. "Violence to Humans and Animals," op. cit.

18. Dr. Randall Lockwood and Guy R. Hodge, op. cit.

19. "Violence to Humans and Animals," op. cit.

20. Dr. Randall Lockwood and Guy R. Hodge, op. cit.

21. "Violence to Humans and Animals," op. cit.

22. Craig Schneider, et al., "Details Shed Little Light on Riddle That Was Mark Barton," *The Atlanta Journal and Constitution*, August 7, 1999, pp. F1, F4.

23. "Youth Violence and Animal Cruelty," op. cit.

24. Ibid.

25. Ibid.

26. Henry Farber and Leon Stafford, "Parents Mystified As to What Set Off Son," *The Atlanta Journal and Constitution*, August 11, 1999, p. E3.

27. Randall Lockwood and Frank R. Ascione, ed., *Cruelty to Animals and Interpersonal Violence* (West Lafayette, IN: Purdue University Press, 1998).

28. Dr. Randall Lockwood and Guy R. Hodge, op. cit.

29. Ibid.

30. Ibid.

31. Michael W. Fox, *Eating With Conscience: The Bioethics of Food* (Troutdale, OR: New Sage Press, 1997).

32. "Choosing a Humane Diet: How to Get Started," The Humane Society of the United States, Washington, DC, 1999.

33. *Circulation: the Journal of the American Heart Association*, July 27, 1999.

34. "Choosing a Humane Diet," op. cit.

35. Ibid.

36. Associated Press, "Soy Proposed As Way to Cut Fat in Kid's Meals," *The Atlanta Constitution*, December 24, 1999.

37. Program, National Town Meeting for a Sustainable America, Henry Ford Museum, Detroit, Michigan, May 3, 1999.

38. Ibid.

39. Ibid.

40. "Choosing a Humane Diet," op. cit.

41. Michael W. Fox, *Eating With Conscience*, op. cit., p. 166.

42. "The Genuine Progress Indicator," Redefining Progress, San Francisco, *Earth Ethics*, Center for Respect of Life and Environment, Washington, DC, Spring/Summer 1996, pp. 24–25.

43. Ibid.

44. Richard M. Clugston, "Critical Tasks for the Earth Charter Process," *Earth Ethics*, Center for Respect of Life and Environment, Washington, DC, Spring/Summer 1996, pp. 17–20, 26.

45. Ibid.

46. Herman E. Daly, "Sustainable Development Is Possible Only If We Forego Growth," *Earth Island Journal*, Spring 1992, p. 12.

47. Peter M. Vitousek, Paul R. Ehrlich, Anne H. Ehrlich, and Pamela A. Matson, "Human Appropriation of the Products of Photosynthesis," *BioScience*, 36: 368–373, 1986.

48. Clifford Cobb and John B. Cobb, *The Green National Product: A Proposed Index of Sustainable Economic Welfare* (Lanham, Maryland: University Press of America, 1994).

49. "The Genuine Progress Indicator," op. cit.

50. World Conservation Union, United Nations Environment Program, and Worldwide Fund for Nature, *Caring for the Earth: A Strategy for Sustainable Living*, United Nations Environment Program, Gland, Switzerland, October 1991.

51. Ibid.

52. Ibid.

53. Ibid.

54. "WTO Fact Sheet," The Humane Society of the United States, Washington, DC, November 1999.

55. "Globalization vs. Nature," Turning Point Project, *The New York Times*, November 22, 1999, p. A15.

56. "Invisible Government," Turning Point Project, *The New York Times*, November 29, 1999, p. A15.

57. "The World Trade Organization and the Environment: A Citizens' Action Guide," Friends of the Earth, Washington, DC, October 1999.

58. "Behind the Hubbub in Seattle," *The New York Times*, December 1, 1999, p. A14.

59. Joseph Kahn, "Seattle Talks Reflect a Burst of Conflicts and Trade Hopes," *The New York Times*, November 1999, pp. A1, A8.

60. "Globalization vs. Nature," op. cit.

61. "Invisible Government," op. cit.

62. Joseph Kahn, op. cit.

63. "The World Trade Organization and Environment," op. cit.

64. "WTO Fact Sheet," op. cit.

65. "Globalization vs. Nature," op. cit.

66. "Invisible Government," op. cit.

67. Joseph Kahn, op. cit.

68. "Globalization vs. Nature," op. cit.

69. "Invisible Government," op. cit.

70. Steven C. Rockefeller, "Global Ethics, International Law, and The Earth Charter," Center for Respect of life and Environment, Washington, DC, Spring/Summer 1996, pp. 1–4.

71. "The Earth Charter: A Global Ethic for the Twenty-First Century," Center for Respect of Life and Environment, Washington, DC, 1999.

72. "Introduction to the Earth Charter Initiative" and "Benchmark Draft II," Earth Charter USA Campaign, Center for Respect of Life and Environment, Washington, DC, April 1999.

73. "The Earth Charter," op. cit.

74. Ibid.

75. Ibid.

76. "Introduction to the Earth Charter Initiative," op. cit.

77. Ibid.

78. Jan Hartke, personal communication, January 2000.

79. Ibid.

80. Ibid.

81. Michael W. Fox, *Inhumane Society*, op. cit.

82. Rachel Carson, *Silent Spring* (New York: Crest Paperback, 1962), p. vii.

83. Bernard Unte, op. cit.

84. Andrew Linzey, *Christianity and the Rights of Animals* (New York: Crossroad, 1987), pp. 148–149.

85. Ibid.

86. Andrew Rowan, personal communication, December 1999.

87. Emily Stewart Leavitt, *Animals and Their Legal Rights* (Washington, DC: Animal Welfare Institute, 1970), pp. 13–14, 17–21.

88. Ibid.

89. Gerald Carson, *Men, Beasts, and Gods* (New York: Charles Scribner's Sons, 1972), pp. 54, 95–120.

90. Ibid.

91. Bernard Unte, op. cit.

92. Ibid.

93. Ibid.

94. Albert Gore, *Earth in the Balance: Ecology and the Human Spirit* (Boston: Houghton-Mifflin, 1992), p. 269.

95. Jan Hartke, op. cit.

96. Ibid.

97. Ibid.

98. *HSUS News*, The Humane Society of the United States, Washington, DC, Spring 1993, pp. 18–20.

99. Richard M. Clugston, "Developing a Workable Earth Ethic," *Earth Ethics*, Center for Respect of Life and Environment, Washington, DC, Spring 1993, pp. 11–12.

100. Marilyn Wilhelm, "All One Family: The Cosmos Is a Kinship System," Address to the National Conference of the Humane Society of the United States, Fort Worth, Texas, October 13, 1983.

101. Thomas Berry, "The Challenge of our Times," *Earth Ethics*, Center for Respect of Life and Environment, Washington, DC, Fall/Winter 1997–1998, pp. 29–32.

102. Michael W. Fox, *The Boundless Circle* (Wheaton, IL: Quest Books, 1996).

103. Ibid.

About the Author

Paul G. Irwin is the President and Chief Executive Officer of The Humane Society of the United States (HSUS). With over 7 million constituents, the HSUS is the nation's largest animal protection organization devoted to promoting the welfare of animals, both wild and domestic.

An officer of The HSUS since 1976, Mr. Irwin was awarded a Doctor of Letters degree from Rio Grande College; earned masters degrees from Boston University and Colgate Rochester Divinity School; and received a baccalaureate from Roberts Wesleyan College. Postgraduate work was completed at Harvard University and the Massachusetts Mental Health Center. Mr. Irwin is an ordained United Methodist clergyman.

During Mr. Irwin's tenure, The HSUS has become a national and global leader in advancing the cause of animal protection. Under his leadership, the society was accepted and continues as an accredited consultative organization at the United Nations, is a participant at the International Whaling Commission and CITES, and has a consultative role with the World Trade Organization. Mr. Irwin was also appointed by President Clinton as an advisor to the Office of the United States Trade Representative.

Mr. Irwin has established a priority program status for several society focuses, including companion animal issues, sustainable agricultural and farm animal protection, immunocontraception of domestic and wild animals, and the rehabilitation and release of orphaned, stranded, and captive animals both marine and terrestrial.

Mr. Irwin serves as President of the World Society for the Protection of Animals headquartered in London, England, EarthVoice, the Center for Respect of Life and the Environment, the International Center for Earth Concerns, and Humane Society International. He serves on the board of directors of the American Bible Society, the Wilhelm Schole, the Renewable Natural Resources Foundation, and the National Association for the Humane and Environmental Education.

INDEX